NEW TESTAMENT GUIDES

General Editor
A.T. Lincoln

LUKE

LUKE

Christopher M. Tuckett

Sheffield Academic Press

Published by Sheffield Academic Press Ltd
Mansion House
19 Kingfield Road
Sheffield, S11 9AS
England

Printed on acid-free paper in Great Britain
by The Cromwell Press
Melksham, Wiltshire

British Library Cataloguing in Publication Data

A catalogue record for this book is available
from the British Library

ISBN 1-85075-751-8

Contents

Contents

Abbreviations

ABD	*Anchor Bible Dictionary*
BBB	Bonner Biblische Beiträge
JBL	*Journal of Biblical Literature*
JSNT	*Journal for the Study of the New Testament*
JSNTSup	*Journal for the Study of the New Testament, Supplement Series*
NIGTC	New International Greek Testament Commentaries
NovTSup	*Novum Testamentum*, Supplement Series
NRSV	New Revised Standard Version
NTS	*New Testament Studies*
SBLDS	SBL Dissertation Series
SBLMS	SBL Monograph Series
SNTSMS	Society of New Testament Studies Monograph Series

All biblical quotations are from the New Revised Standard Version unless otherwise stated.

Commentaries and General Works on Luke's Gospel

Commentaries on the text of Luke's gospel are many and varied. Some of the following are specifically based on the English text, some on the Greek; however, most of the latter can be studied profitably by those without a knowledge of Greek, while several of those ostensibly based on the English text refer to Greek at times. No attempt has therefore been made in what follows to divide the commentaries into two lists. All the secondary literature cited here is restricted to works written in English.

G.B. Caird, *The Gospel of St Luke* (Pelican New Testament Commentaries; Harmondsworth: Penguin Books, 1963).

J.M. Creed, *The Gospel according to St Luke* (Macmillan: London, 1930). A classic study based on the Greek text.

E.E. Ellis, *The Gospel of Luke* (New Century Bible; London: Marshall, Morgan & Scott, 1974). Based on the English text and of medium length: careful and thorough exegesis.

C.F. Evans, *Saint Luke* (TPI New Testament Commentaries; London: SCM Press, 1990). Based on the English text. Very long and detailed.

J.A. Fitzmyer, *The Gospel according to Luke* (Anchor Bible; 2 vols.; Doubleday: New York, 1981, 1985). An extremely thorough and invaluable treatment, with a monograph length introduction on Luke. A standard work.

M.D. Goulder, *Luke—A New Paradigm* (JSNTSup, 20; Sheffield: JSOT Press, 1989). In the form of a commentary, but focusing primarily on the question of Luke's sources, and advocating the theory that Luke is dependent on Matthew.

I.H. Marshall, *The Gospel of Luke* (NIGTC; Exeter: Paternoster, 1979). Very full and clear, though with a tendency to concentrate on questions of historicity.

J. Nolland, *The Gospel of Luke* (3 vols.; Word Biblical Commentaries; Dallas: Word Books, 1990–94). Very full coverage.

R.C. Tannehill, *The Narrative Unity of Luke–Acts: A Literary Interpretation. I. The Gospel according to Luke* (Philadelphia: Fortress Press, 1986). A fine literary analysis of the gospel.

Other works on Luke dealing with a range of critical issues:

C.K. Barrett, *Luke the Historian in Recent Study* (London: Epworth, 1961). An excellent, concise survey.

F. Bovon, *Luke the Theologian. Thirty-three Years of Research (1950–83)* (trans. A. Park: Pickwick Press, 1987). The French original covers up to 1975; the appendix, covering more recent material, is very cryptic. The quality of the English translation is also not easy at times.

H.J. Cadbury, *The Making of Luke–Acts* (Macmillan: New York, 1927; repr. London: SPCK, 1968). A classic study.

H. Conzelmann, *The Theology of Saint Luke* (ET; London: Faber, 1960). Again a classic, in many ways inaugurating modern Lukan studies.

F.W. Danker, *Luke* (Proclamation Commentaries; Philadelphia: Fortress Press, 1976). Concise treatment of a range of issues in study of Luke.

P.F. Esler, *Community and Gospel in Luke–Acts* (SNTSMS, 57; Cambridge: Cambridge University Press, 1987). A powerful analysis, useful too for showing the ways in which sociological insights can assist exegesis.

J.A. Fitzmyer, *Luke the Theologian: Aspects of his Teaching* (New York: Paulist Press, 1989). Effectively a supplement to his commentary.

E. Franklin, *Christ the Lord. A Study in the Purpose and Theology of Luke–Acts* (London: SPCK, 1975). A general study of many aspects of Lukan theology.

D. Juel, *Luke–Acts: The Promise of History* (Atlanta: John Knox, 1983). A brief and clear study of key Lukan themes.

R. Maddox, *The Purpose of Luke–Acts* (Edinburgh: T. & T. Clark, 1982). An excellent treatment of many of the topics discussed in this book.

I.H. Marshall, *Luke: Historian and Theologian* (Exeter: Paternoster Press, 1970). Clear and incisive discussion of all the main themes in contemporary Lukan study by a renowned Lukan specialist.

I.H. Marshall, *The Acts of the Apostles* (New Testament Guides; Sheffield: JSOT Press, 1992). A companion to the present volume in the same series, covering a range of topics in study of Acts.

E. Schweizer, *Luke: A Challenge to Present Theology* (London: SPCK, 1982). A brief survey of Luke with an eye to contemporary theology.

The following collections of essays are also important:

L.E. Keck and J.L. Martyn (eds.), *Studies in Luke–Acts* (Nashville: Abingdon, 1966; repr. London: SPCK, 1968). A classic set of essays.

C.H. Talbert (ed.), *Perspectives on Luke–Acts* (Edinburgh: T. & T. Clark, 1978).

J.B. Tyson (ed.), *Luke–Acts and the Jewish People. Eight Critical Perspectives* (Minneapolis: Augsburg, 1988). Showing the variety of different views on this topic.

J.H. Neyrey (ed.), *The Social World of Luke–Acts* (Peabody: Hendrickson, 1991). An important collection showing some of the ways in which application of the social sciences can aid interpretation of the text.

Other works related to the topics covered in the individual chapters are listed at the end of each chapter.

1

INTRODUCTION

THE GOSPEL OF LUKE raises many problems for any contemporary interpreter. In one sense such a claim is of course trite: any ancient text written almost two thousand years ago raises problems for anyone who wants to try to understand it. There are, for example, problems of language: Luke's Gospel is written in Greek, a language which for many of us is not our own. We need therefore to be able to translate Luke's Greek into a language which we can understand. Yet even that process is by no means simple or straightforward. Even if we can work out what the individual words, or perhaps sentences, mean at one level, we often have to undergo a potentially complex and prolonged process of seeking to understand the background, the social and cultural conventions within which the text operates, if we are to understand it in more than the most superficial of senses. We can, for example, understand the meaning of the words of parables such as the Good Samaritan (Lk. 10.30-35) or the Pharisee and the tax-collector (Lk. 18.10-14) by translating them into English or by reading the parables in a modern English translation. But unless we know something about Samaritans, Pharisees or tax-collectors, we shall probably miss large parts of the meaning. Similarly, we can read the parable of the Great Supper (Lk. 14.16-24) at one level in English translation; but without some idea of the social conventions of the first century—about the nature of meals, the conventions of invitations, the possible background of the excuses made by the original guests etc.—we shall miss parts of the meaning, or, worse, misinterpret the parable by reading in anachronistically our own twentieth century presuppositions and conventions into the story. Thus in order to understand any text we need to know something of its literary, cultural and historical context to be able to understand it more than just superficially.

In relation to biblical texts, many of the broader issues of general cultural and historical background are dealt with in other textbooks. However, with any text, we also need to know something of the particular circumstances of its composition and indeed of its very nature: Who wrote it? For whom? Why was it written? And what kind of a text is it trying to be? Many of these questions in biblical study come under the broad rubric of 'Introduction', and it is with some of these introductory problems that we shall be concerned in this first chapter.

The interpretation of one of the New Testament Gospels does, however, raise even more complex issues than is the case with some other texts from antiquity, or even from the New Testament. The Gospels all purport to be historical (at least in a loose sense) accounts of events that have taken place prior to the time of the writer: they are all accounts of some parts of the life, passion and death of Jesus, with at least some kind of sequel, however small, of what was claimed to follow his death. There are then at least two possible ways of approaching a text like a Gospel: do we use it to try to understand something about the history being described? Or do we use it to try to discover something about the person who wrote it? Such a distinction is, of course, far too simplistic since there are many shades of grey between the two extremes I have just mentioned, as there are also other possibilities. Yet the two can perhaps serve to focus the discussion here: do we seek to use a text like the Gospel of Luke to tell us something about Jesus, or about Luke?

It is probably fair to say that the vast bulk of contemporary study of the Gospel of Luke today, if faced with such a choice, opts for the latter and not the former. If we want to discover information about Jesus, Luke's Gospel may be one of our sources, but it will certainly not be our only one, and some might argue not our main one. As we shall see shortly,

Luke's Gospel is almost certainly not the first Gospel to be written and hence is not closest in time to the events being described. That is not to say that Luke's Gospel does not have any contribution to make to our knowledge about Jesus: many of the best-known parables of Jesus are found in Luke's Gospel, and it is the parabolic teaching of Jesus that has often been thought most characteristic of Jesus. Nevertheless, the dominant trend in modern study of the Gospels has been to focus on the particularity of each Gospel and to see what that might tell us about its writer and the circumstances in which and for which it was written, quite as much as seeking to unravel the history it describes.

This is something of a change from the past, certainly in relation to the so-called Synoptic Gospels (i.e. Matthew, Mark and Luke, as opposed to John). A tradition as early as Clement of Alexandria (early third century CE) contrasted John with the other Gospels, saying that whilst the latter presented the 'bodily things' (probably meaning a reasonably straight factual history), John 'wrote a spiritual Gospel'. And in the nineteenth and early twentieth centuries, scholars expended much energy on sorting out the relationships between the three Synoptic Gospels, primarily with a view to rediscovering the history which they described. In the early part of the twentieth century, attention shifted to the traditions which the evangelists had used, and scholars focused on the ways in which these smaller units of tradition had been handed on and used in the early church. (This discipline was known as form criticism.) In this, the evangelists were often regarded as simply editors, people who stitched together the individual stories or units of the tradition in a fairly mechanical way.

However, in the second half of the twentieth century, this view of the matter has changed significantly. The evangelists are seen no longer as mechanical editors, cutting and pasting material without too much thought. Rather, they have come to be seen as theologians (at least in some sense) in their own right, with their own particular theological agendas and their own distinctive ideas which have significantly influenced the ways in which they have told their story about Jesus. No longer is there such a qualitative line implicitly

drawn between John and the Synoptics: rather, all have
written in some sense 'spiritual' Gospels, that is, accounts
which are not *just* dry recitals of physical facts (though what
ever is?!), but accounts which are deeply impregnated by the
concerns and beliefs of their authors. Further, in recent
years it has been increasingly recognized that just as important as any theological ideas of a writer are the *social* factors
in any situation which may significantly affect the way in
which an author writes. Anyway it is the attempt to find out
what these concerns and factors are that dominates so much
of Gospel studies today. (The technical term for this is redaction criticism, which we shall discuss in a little more detail
later.) Such an approach is the one which will be adopted
here. Thus in what follows, I shall be trying to consider
primarily what we can discover about Luke, his concerns and
his ideas, and not so much about Jesus and the events which
Luke describes.

However, in the case of Luke's Gospel, there is a further
complicating factor, one which is in one way a great advan-
tage, but also one which makes life more complex. This is the
fact that, by almost universal consent today, the Gospel
which we now call the Gospel of Luke is part of a two-volume
work: the author of Luke's Gospel also wrote a sequel to his
Gospel, namely the Acts of the Apostles. As far as we know
Luke was unique in this. No one else thought that his Gospel
account should be continued with an extended history of the
early church. All this means that if we are to try to discover
something about the special features of Luke's Gospel with a
view to discovering Luke's own concerns, we simply cannot
ignore Acts. Acts itself sometimes gives us insight into
specific features of Luke's special concerns and situation; but
even its very existence is significant.

This creates a slight tension in the present context. On the
one hand, we have to take full account of Acts in assessing
Luke and his concerns. On the other hand, the present small
volume is intended as an introduction to Luke's Gospel, and
many of the features of Acts are discussed in Professor
Marshall's excellent treatment of that book in this series
(Marshall 1992). The present book thus has to try to strike a
balance between seeking to do justice to Luke and his work,

which must include Acts as well as the Gospel, and seeking
to focus primarily on the Gospel.

No doubt each reader of Luke's Gospel would strike that
balance differently. For better or worse, I have decided to try
to take significant account of the evidence provided by Acts
at relevant points in the discussion of the various topics
considered here. Nevertheless, the fact that primary focus is
on the Gospel does mean that the evidence of Acts will generally not be treated as fully as the evidence from the Gospel,
and that some topics, of prime significance in the interpretation of Acts rather than the Gospel, will be discussed only
briefly here. For example, the question of authorship, which I
shall consider shortly, is probably of far less significance in
relation to the Gospel than it is in relation to Acts.
Nevertheless, we cannot ignore Acts in any assessment of
what Luke's concerns were, and so inevitably we shall have
to draw the evidence of Acts into the discussion at times.

In the present chapter I shall look at some of the so-called
introductory problems of Luke's Gospel before going on to
look at some of the most characteristic features of his ideas,
as well as some of the problems of contemporary Lukan
studies, in subsequent chapters. A small book like this
cannot hope to provide a comprehensive coverage of Luke's
leading ideas or of the social factors influencing Luke. Thus I
have chosen to focus on a smaller number of key areas to try
to illustrate important aspects of Luke's Gospel. Those who
are interested can find more extended treatments of Lukan
theology, and wider coverage, in the further reading
suggested in the bibliographies.

Author

One 'introductory' problem frequently raised in relation to
many ancient texts is that of authorship. By tradition, we
always call the third Gospel the 'Gospel of Luke'. But both
the Gospel itself and Acts are anonymous. Nowhere does the
author explicitly say who he is. (However, the Lukan writings are significantly different from some other texts in that
the author does explicitly refer to himself and his work in the
prologues in Lk. 1.1-4 and Acts 1.1. The problem of the so-

called 'we-passages' in Acts, where the narrative slips into the first person plural, is more debated and complex.) What then can we way about the author of our Gospel?

In one way the question is probably not very important in the interpretation of the Gospel, and the issue is probably more pressing in relation to Acts. It is universally agreed that the tradition naming the author of this two-volume work as 'Luke' is identifying him with the person mentioned occasionally in the Pauline corpus as a member of Paul's entourage (Phlm. 24; Col. 4.14; 2 Tim. 4.11. The social set-up of the time makes it almost certain that the author was a man: I shall therefore refer to him as male, rather than use 'him/her'.). There has been fierce debate abut the accuracy of this identification. If correct, it would make the author a companion of Paul and hence (presumably) an eye-witness of at least some (though only some) of the events described in Acts. The interpretation of the we-passages is clearly relevant here: is the author here indicating that he was an active participant in the events described? The debate is so fierce partly because there are a number of discrepancies, or inconsistencies, at many levels between the picture of Paul in Acts and the picture of Paul which emerges from his letters. Hence the question arises of how accurate the account of Paul in the second half of Acts really is.

There is, however, more than one issue involved here. Whether the author was an eye-witness of (some) events of Paul's career, and whether he reported Paul accurately, are two rather different matters. We could quite happily answer yes or no to either question quite independently of the other: the author could have been an inaccurate eye-witness, or a highly accurate non-eye-witness!

But whatever we decide, the issues are probably of little relevance to the study of the Gospel itself. The author of the Gospel seems to distinguish himself in his prologue from eye-witnesses of the events he describes (Lk. 1.2). He may even be indicating too that he belongs to a third generation of Christianity: it is unclear how the 'servants of the word' of 1.2 relate to the 'eye-witnesses'; but it seems clear that Luke is not a direct participant in the events about to be described in his Gospel.

In part too this also depends on the precise interpretation of another much disputed word in the Lukan prologue, namely the assertion by Luke that he has 'investigated' (so NRSV, Greek *parēkolouthēkoti*) everything 'carefully' (Greek *akribōs*). The verb has sometimes been interpreted as implying that Luke actually participated in the events concerned (so Cadbury 1922: 502). However, such a meaning seems unlikely in view of the claim that Luke had done this to 'everything'; moreover, 'carefully' is a very odd adverb to use in this context if a claim of active participation is being made. Hence most would interpret the verb as the NRSV translates, that is, as 'investigate', or 'make oneself familiar' (cf. Alexander 1993: 128-30).

I shall therefore continue to call our author Luke simply for convenience sake if nothing else, without prejudging one way or the other the issue of whether this Luke is the same Luke as the person mentioned in the Pauline corpus.

Date

Partly connected with the authorship question is the problem of the date of Luke–Acts. This issue is also potentially connected with the problem of the purpose of Acts, and hence insofar as Acts is part of the whole of Luke–Acts, with the purpose of Luke's Gospel as well. As is well known, the second half of Acts is dominated by the activity of Paul, with the last quarter of the book taken up with Paul's journey to Rome as a prisoner facing trial. Acts ends, however, without ever telling the reader the outcome of Paul's trial. This has led some to argue that Paul's trial may not yet have taken place by the time Acts was written: hence Acts, and perhaps Luke–Acts, is to be dated in the early 60s.

This seems implausible. It is possible, but not likely, that Luke's Gospel was written after Acts: the present form of the prologues certainly suggests that the two books are conceived of as a unity right from the start. In fact most scholars would wish to date Luke–Acts after the fall of Jerusalem in 70 CE. Luke himself states that he has had predecessors in writing a Gospel account (Lk. 1.1), and one such predecessor is almost certainly the author of the Gospel we call Mark (cf.

below). Mark's Gospel is probably to be dated in the late 60s or early 70s, and hence Luke's Gospel must be after this. Other evidence would also seem to point to a date after 70 CE. For example, at one point Luke rewrites the prediction of Mark's Jesus of a terrible calamity to arise: in Mk 13.14 Mark's Jesus speaks of 'the desolating sacrilege set up where it ought not to be', using language applied to the desecration of the temple in the book of Daniel (cf. Dan. 9.27). Luke rewrites this to read 'When you see Jerusalem surrounded by armies...' (Lk. 21.20), and seems clearly to interpret the enigmatic Markan verse in terms of the fall of Jerusalem in 70 CE. Similarly the prediction of Jesus in Lk. 19.43 of Jerusalem ('The days will come upon you, when your enemies will set up ramparts around you and surround you, and hem you in on every side') looks very much as if it is written after the siege of Jerusalem, with moderately precise knowledge of exactly what happened then (even if some more general prophecy of the destruction of the city may be traced back to Jesus). Hence a date after 70 seems most plausible. (Further, whatever one makes of the ending of Acts, it seems unlikely that Acts is written before Paul's trial has happened: the prediction of Luke's Paul to the Ephesian elders in Acts 20.25, that 'none of you...will ever see my face again', is widely regarded as a clear hint that Luke does know that Paul was executed and is now dead.)

How much after 70 Luke–Acts is to be dated is more uncertain and a wide variety of possible dates has been proposed. O'Neill (1970) suggests quite a late date, that is, into the second century, on the basis of affinities between Luke and apologists like Justin. This, however, seems difficult to maintain. As we shall see, Luke has a relatively positive attitude to the state authorities; and such an attitude is difficult to conceive by c. 125 CE when, as far as we can tell, profession of the Christian faith became an offence automatically punishable by death. (Cf. the correspondence between Pliny, governor of Bithynia, and the Emperor Trajan.) Luke's positive and irenic view of the state authorities seems to be more at home in the first century than in the second. Thus a date at some period in the last quarter of the first century seems most likely, though it is probably impossible to be more precise.

Text

A brief word needs perhaps to be said here about the text of Luke's Gospel. We do not, of course, have Luke's own autograph copy of the text he wrote. We only have copies of copies of the text, made at a later date. The earliest manuscripts of the text of Luke–Acts come on papyrus from the early third century, and the text in full Bibles from the fourth century onwards.

For the most part, the lack of an autograph of any New Testament book is rarely felt to be problematic. There will always be debates about some details, but the text is generally thought to be reasonably well established so that we can in practice be fairly confident that our modern text in a critical edition of the Greek New Testament is not so far removed from the 'original'.

The Lukan writings do, however, pose a number of peculiar text-critical problems. There is not enough space to do more than scratch the surface of the discipline of textual criticism here. But, very broadly speaking, the earliest manuscripts of the New Testament can be divided into two groups, one usually called Alexandrian, and the other Western. Again, very broadly speaking, the Alexandrian tradition has often been felt to be more reliable and a better witness to the original text; the Western text tends to embellish and add details or a variety of reasons.

Now the difference between these two major textual traditions is often relatively small, though for some reason, there is a far greater difference between the two textual traditions in the text of Acts. In itself that is a problem for the study of Acts and will therefore be left on one side here. However, the textual tradition of Luke's Gospel also shows a number of significant differences between the two main textual traditions. In particular there are a number of places where the Western text (represented above all by the manuscript Codex Bezae, usually known as D) is shorter than the Alexandrian text. Since the tendency of the Western text is usually to amplify and add elements to the text, it has been thought by some in the past that these Western readings could be original (since the Western text's tendency is to expand, not to

contract). These texts, sometimes called (sadly and somewhat tendentiously) 'Western non-interpolations', have
aroused much discussion.

For a reason which is by no means clear, these Western
non-interpolations seem to cluster in the Lukan passion narrative. To mention three of the most famous, there is the
reference to Jesus' ascension, apparently on the first Easter
day, in Lk. 24.51 (omitted by D, though also with some support from one major Alexandrian manuscript, codex
Sinaiticus), the note about Peter running to the tomb and
finding it empty in Lk. 24.12, and perhaps the most perplexing of all the textual variants, almost (but not quite) all of
Jesus' words of institution at the Last Supper in Lk. 22.19b-
20, so that codex D has Jesus just take bread and say 'This is
my body', with no more interpretation of the bread and also
no reference to taking the cup and interpreting it/its
contents. One other notable textual variant comes in Lk.
23.34 where several manuscripts (not just Western ones)
omit Jesus' words praying for forgiveness for his executioners.

There is no space to discuss the issue in detail here. The
tendency in recent years has probably been to discount these
Western readings as having no value. Thus while in older
editions of the Greek New Testament, and in older English
translations (e.g. the Revised Version), the shorter (Western)
reading was often taken as the text, and the longer
(Alexandrian) reading either bracketed in the text or con-
signed to a footnote, the trend more recently has been to read
the fuller, longer reading as the genuine text of the Gospel,
and to mention the variant shorter reading only in a footnote
(if indeed at all).

Perhaps each case has to be considered on its own merits;
but the texts are potentially significant in a number of ways.
For example, Lk. 24.12, if part of the text of Luke, provides a
notable feature paralleling Luke and John. Lk. 22.19b-20
raises the question of whether Jesus' death is the inaugura-
tion of a *new* covenant relationship (the reference is precisely
in the disputed v. 20). One should therefore be at least aware
of the text-critical problems associated with Luke's Gospel.

Sources

If we are concerned above all to discover something of Luke's own concerns, how should we proceed? One way which has been very much in vogue in the past has been to look at the way in which Luke uses and changes his sources. If that is the case, then it is vital to know what sources Luke used in his Gospel. (The problem of the possible sources used in Acts will not be discussed here.)

The whole question of Luke's sources is a complex one for which there is again not space enough to discuss in detail here. (For fuller treatments, see Fitzmyer 1970; Tuckett 1992.) Luke's Gospel is one of the Synoptic Gospels (Matthew, Mark and Luke), so-called because they are so similar to each other in many ways, in wording and in order, that they can usefully be viewed together. (The Greek preposition *syn* means together, 'optic' means looking at.) When one does this, it becomes apparent that the similarity between all three is too close to be coincidental. (If one needs any counter example to show that not every Gospel must have been written this way, one has only to glance at the fourth Gospel.) Hence it seems most likely that the three are in some kind of literary relationship with each other: one Gospel writer has used one or more of the others, or the evangelists have had access to common sources. Trying to sort out the nature of these dependencies is known as the Synoptic Problem.

We may perhaps distinguish two aspects of the problem: broadly the agreements between the Gospels may be divided into material where all three are parallel to each other, and material where only two are, and in the latter case this is almost always Matthew and Luke.

Mark

In the case of material which is in Mark as well as the others, the standard solution today is that Mark's Gospel was the source used by both Matthew and Luke independently. The detailed reasons can be found elsewhere (see Streeter 1924; Fitzmyer 1970), and it should also be noted that this is by no means a universally held view: a small but

powerful minority of scholars (e.g. Farmer 1964) would hold
that the agreements between Mark and Matthew/Luke are
better explained if Mark came last, combining both Matthew
and Luke (the so-called 'Griesbach hypothesis'). However, the
majority have remained unconvinced, not least because it is
hard to see any very good reason why Mark would have been
produced if Matthew and Luke were already in existence:
virtually everything in Mark is in either Matthew or Luke or
both. On the other hand, the reverse situation seems very
much more plausible. Mark's Gospel is shorter; and Matthew
and Luke, if written later, may have wanted to supplement
Mark with extra material they had available. Similarly,
many of the detailed changes in both wording and order are
relatively easy to envisage if Mark came first, and much
harder to envisage happening in reverse if Mark came last.
Thus I shall assume here the theory that Luke used Mark as
one of his sources.

Q

Luke also shares a lot of material with Matthew alone. The
solution to this aspect of the Synoptic Problem is more disputed. The standard solution today is that Matthew and
Luke do not depend on each other, but both have used a
common source, now lost, called Q. However, the nature of Q,
and the fact that Q (if it existed) is now lost, has always
caused difficulty for many. Thus some have argued that Q
was never a single source but only a collection of possibly
disparate material which never existed together before being
used by Matthew and Luke; others have argued that Q never
existed at all and that the agreements between Matthew and
Luke are to be explained by Luke's direct dependence on
Matthew (so above all Goulder 1989, as well as advocates of
the Griesbach hypothesis).

Again there is no space for a detailed discussion here.
Suffice it to say that, despite the arguments of Goulder and
others, the theory of Luke's dependence on Matthew has not
carried the day. Above all, such a theory would have to
account for a radically greater freedom by Luke in relation to
Matthew's ordering of events than is the case in relation to
Luke's use of Markan material (where Luke very rarely

changes the Markan order); further, Luke must have studiously ignored all of Matthew's additions to Mark in Markan material (cf. Mt. 16.16-19, added by Matthew to Mark, but Luke shows no awareness of it). Further, most have argued that neither Matthew nor Luke has any monopoly on the more original form of the tradition in the material they share in common: sometimes Matthew seems to be more original; but equally often, if not more so, Luke seems to be more original (cf. Lk. 6.20-21; 11.2-4; 11.49; 12.8 etc. For detailed discussion of individual texts, see Catchpole 1993, ch. 1; more generally Tuckett 1995). This combination of part–negative, part-positive arguments have convinced many that Luke did not know Matthew, and hence both depend on common source material(s), usually known as Q. The precise nature of Q is perhaps then a further question which need not concern us here.

The position taken in the rest of this book will be then the so-called Two Source Theory, the two main sources (of Matthew and Luke) being Mark and Q.

Proto-Luke

It is clear that Markan and Q material does not cover the whole of Luke's Gospel. Luke contains a substantial body of material which is peculiar to his Gospel. This includes the birth stories (Lk. 1–2) as well as many of the best known parables in the Gospels (the Good Samaritan, the Prodigal Son, the Rich Man and Lazarus etc.), and this material is usually known as L. Whether L ever existed in written form prior to Luke's Gospel is very uncertain. The L material may simply consist of isolated sayings and traditions which Luke had at his disposal but which may have come to him from a variety of different origins.

There is, however, one theory concerning L which has been fashionable in the past, though less popular today, and which should perhaps be mentioned briefly here. This is the so-called Proto-Luke theory. This argues that, although L alone may never have existed in written form, the material Q + L together may have done. Luke may have written a first draft of his Gospel using the Q + L material; subsequently he came across Mark's Gospel, and added the material from this to his existing draft, adding too at this stage perhaps the birth narratives. It is this earlier version of Luke, a Proto-Luke, which may lie behind our present Gospel (so Streeter 1924; Taylor 1926; Caird 1963).

The theory is possible, but scarcely provable. It is true that the birth narratives may have been added at a slightly later stage: Lk. 3.1 looks as if it could have been an original opening of a book, and the genealogy in Lk. 3.23-28 would then come immediately after the first mention of Jesus. (In the present form of the Gospel the genealogy seems to come very late.) So too Luke's Gospel is notable for the way in which Markan and non-Markan material seems to come in large, alternating blocks.

Yet while the evidence can be explained by a Proto-Luke theory, it by no means demands such a theory. The birth narratives do play a key role in Luke's presentation and can scarcely be relegated to the status of an afterthought. The block phenomenon could be adequately explained just as well if Luke were inserting Q + L material into Mark, rather than vice versa. And in any case, some at least of the present Q + L material seems to show vestiges of Markan influence (e.g. Lk. 4.23; 12.10; 17.31); at the very least one would then have to allow for Luke having touched up his Proto-Luke here and there. In the end the theory is probably untestable and ultimately not very useful. The Q + L material clearly comes from a variety of sources and it is not clear how much is gained by positing an earlier form of Luke's Gospel as having combined them.

Passion Narrative
There is, however, one part of the source problem that is more uncertain, and this concerns the passion narrative in Luke. It is widely agreed that Q did not contain a passion narrative: Matthew seems to show no knowledge of any major source other than Mark in his version of the passion. Luke's relationship to Mark here, however, is very unclear. Certainly it is doubtful how far Luke used Mark as his source for the passion narrative. The verbal agreement between Luke and Mark drops quite sharply (from over 50 per cent in the rest of the Gospel to under 30 per cent in the

passion narrative); and whereas in the rest of the Gospel Luke hardly ever changes the Markan order, there are suddenly about 12 (albeit small) differences in order between Luke and Mark in the passion narrative. All this has led a number of scholars to suggest that Luke may have used another source for the passion. And in view of the supreme importance for many of the accounts of Jesus' death, the source-critical question here is of considerable significance (see Streeter 1924; Taylor 1972 and others; the issue is reviewed in R.E. Brown, *The Death of the Messiah* [New York: Doubleday, 1994], pp. 64-75.)

The historical issue is undoubtedly extremely important. However, in the present context, I shall not pursue the matter further. How much all this may tell us about Luke himself is not quite so clear. But to consider this we need to look at the question of methodology in so-called redaction criticism.

Redaction Criticism: Methods and Approaches

The broad aim of redaction criticism (at least as I defined it earlier) is to discover something about the author's own concerns and ideas. How then does one proceed in this?

One of the classic ways in which this has been done in the past has been by considering the ways in which an author has *changed* his sources. (Indeed that is where the phrase 'redaction criticism' comes from: the technical word for 'changing' is 'redacting'.) By looking at the changes Luke has made to Mark, and perhaps to Q if we can recover the Q wording with sufficient certainty, we may be able to see something of Luke's own concerns and interests. Thus, for example, in the next chapter, we shall be looking at some of the changes Luke has made to Mark as revealing perhaps something about his eschatological views.

Such an approach is valid in principle. It is, however, open to one or two cautionary qualifications. Clearly such an approach is heavily dependent on the correct identification of Luke's sources. As we have seen, there is some debate about all aspects of the source theory adopted here, namely the Two Source Theory. Hence, if Luke in fact used Matthew, his

changes to Matthew would look rather different from the
changes he made to the supposed Q source (unless of course
Q was identical with Matthew at every point!); correspond-
ingly the picture that emerges of Luke's redactional activity,
and hence of his major interests and concerns, would look
rather different. All of this may, however, simply indicate the
provisional nature of any conclusions we can draw in a discipline such as Biblical Studies.

There are, however, more serious problems in relation to
the method of redaction criticism as defined just now. First,
the actual changes Luke makes to the wording of his sources
may not be the only way he imposes his ideas on his material. The way in which the material is arranged and structured within the present narrative may also be revealing.
Sometimes this may be by changing the order of one of his
sources; but it might equally be by the way in which different
sources are combined to create a wider literary unity.

Secondly, there is the phenomenon of the material which
Luke may have taken over from his sources without any
change at all. If we only focus on the positive changes Luke
has made to his sources, such material will be ignored.
However, a moment's thought should reveal the inappropri-
ateness of this. If Luke decided to include something from
one of his sources in his Gospel, this may well have been
precisely because he liked it and agreed with it wholeheart-
edly. Indeed the presumption must surely be that this is the
case, unless we have compelling reason for thinking otherwise: if he did not like it, he could presumably simply have
omitted it.

In the light of these difficulties, many scholars today would
therefore argue that seeking to discover Luke's concerns only
via his redaction in the strict sense, that is, by focusing on
the changes he has made to his tradition, will give us a
potentially lop-sided view of Luke. Rather, we should
combine this with a more literary approach, taking seriously
all the material Luke has included as potentially giving us
insight into his ideas. Thus we should look at the structure of
the whole of Luke's work, and the totality of his finished
literary product, quite as much as comparing Luke with his
sources via a synopsis. Further, if we consider Luke's

readers, rather than Luke, such an approach makes much more sense. Luke's initial readers presumably did not have the luxury of a Greek Synopsis available to them. They *may* have known Mark's Gospel, but it seems highly unlikely that they knew it in sufficient detail to have been aware of the instances where Luke was actively changing his Markan source, at least in some of the small ways which redaction critics have noted in the past. They will have been aware primarily of the finished product of Luke's Gospel itself, whether heard or read. Thus any message they may have got will have been that produced by the present form of the literary work as it now stands.

Some would even go so far as to argue that a literary approach is the only legitimate approach, and that we should bracket off the question of sources completely. Certainly one Lukan specialist has written a two-volume analysis—virtually a commentary—on Luke–Acts from this perspective, emphasizing the narrative unity of the whole in its present form and the ways in which the different parts of the narrative cohere with each other (Tannehill 1986).

Perhaps a balanced approach can be maintained, seeking in one way to use the insights provided by source criticism so that Luke's changes to his traditions can be taken into account; but this needs to be balanced by a literary, holistic approach, considering Luke's narrative as a literary whole in its own right, irrespective of where it has come from. Indeed hopefully the two approaches should support each other and produce similar results. Conversely, if a literary approach produces a radically different picture from that of a redactional (i.e. changes-based) approach, then this may indicate that there is something amiss.

As one illustration of a more holistic approach, we may glance briefly at the so-called 'Travel Narrative' in Luke. For whatever reason, Luke has a long section in his Gospel (Lk. 9.51–18.14) of mostly non-Markan material to do with Jesus' teaching which Luke clearly places in the context of a journey to Jerusalem (cf. the very heavy stylized language introducing this in 9.51, and the reminders of the journey context in 13.22; 17.11). It is of course a moot point whether this comes under the rubric of a change to Mark

(Luke interrupting the Markan sequence to insert such a lot of material) or a structural feature of Luke's narrative unity. But either way it is an important feature of Luke's Gospel.

Quite what its significance is for Luke is not certain. It could just be a convenient literary device for Luke to include a lot of teaching material which he has available and has to put in somewhere in his outline. This is possible, though this does not easily explain why the journey motif itself is stressed so much. Some have sought to explain the detailed structure of the Travel Narrative, for example, by (at times quite complex) chiastic structures, or by seeing parallels between Luke's narrative and the book of Deuteronomy, so that Jesus is perhaps being presented as a new prophet like Moses. The fact then that the Travel Narrative may have Christological significance for Luke means that we shall consider it again when we look at the question of Luke's Christology (see Chapter 4 below). But it is perhaps enough to note here that a concentration on the detailed changes in wording alone that Luke makes to his sources may leave important pieces of data untouched in any search for Luke's own concerns and ideas.

Purpose

Why then did Luke write? The question of purpose is often one of the questions brought up in any introductory discussion. In relation to a text like Luke's Gospel it is, however, not really answerable in either abstract or concrete terms at the start of a discussion of the Gospel. Luke's particular purpose is only likely to emerge once we have discovered something of his particular concerns. For those concerns are almost certainly in part a reflection of his purpose in writing.

On the other hand, we do have a statement (albeit brief) of Luke's purpose from Luke himself: in his prologue to the Gospel (Lk. 1.1-4) Luke states something of his purpose in writing, in part reiterated in his prologue to Acts (Acts 1.1).

This prologue to the Gospel has been analysed in great detail on many occasions. It is written in relatively high-class Greek and seems to indicate both Luke's actual credentials and what Luke would like others to think of his credentials.

(The two are not necessarily identical!) The standard critical opinion today is that Luke is here laying claim to be a *historian*. Parallels have been drawn between Luke's prologues in the Gospel and in Acts and similar prologues in the works of historians such as Herodotus, Thucydides, Josephus and others. The prologues of the two volumes of Jospehus's *Contra Apionem* are often thought to be particularly close to Luke's two prologues in his own two-volume work. With this in mind, many have argued that Luke is laying claim, via his prologues, to have his work considered as that of a historian.

This conclusion has been questioned to some extent recently by Loveday Alexander's detailed study of the Lukan prologues (Alexander 1993). She rightly draws attention to a number of differences between the Lukan prologues and those of other contemporary historians. For example, Luke's prologues are much shorter, their style is not really comparable to that of the Hellenistic historians, Luke does not give us his own name, as do most of the historians (using the third person), and the dedication to Theophilus is unlike the normal practice of historians. By contrast, Alexander finds far closer parallels between Luke's prologues and those of so-called scientific treatises so that Luke's books belong within a rather more 'middle-brow' literature within which biography was possible.

All this is well said. On the other hand, as Marshall has pointed out, whatever the formal similarities may imply, the *contents* of Luke–Acts surely place the work more closely in the realm of a history than anything else (Marshall 1992: 21-22). We should also remember the firm attempt to anchor the events being described within the broad sweep of world history in Lk. 2.1; 3.1. Alexander's analysis shows that Luke may not have been considered by others at the time to have been quite so comparable to other great Hellenistic historians of the period; and indeed the modern high evaluation of Luke's rhetorical and literary ability may need considerable revision. Nevertheless, it still remains the case that Luke may be staking a claim to be writing some kind of history and to be accepted as a historian.

We must, however, be careful how much we deduce from

Luke

this, and we should remember that Luke was a first-century writer, not a twentieth century one. Hence we should not judge Luke's worth as a historian by anachronistic criteria. Some have in the past perhaps tried to do this. For example, taken up with issues of historical factual accuracy, many have sought to judge Luke on this basis, and on this basis different conclusions have been reached. Especially in relation to Acts, it has been shown that Luke is at times remarkably accurate in some of the details he records of the cities of the Empire visited by the Christian mission. (For example, the civic leaders in Thessalonica are called politarchs in Acts 17.6, a term which would have been applicable to only a very few cities of the time, but would have been correct in Thessalonica.) On the other hand, several details of Luke's account of Paul's mission do not tally with the evidence of Paul's own letters. Sometimes too Luke's chronology is suspect (cf. the well-known crux in Lk. 2.1 where Luke apparently dates the census to the times when Quirinius was governor of Syria, i.e. c. 6 CE, well after the time of Herod [cf. Lk. 1.5 and Mt. 1–2] who died in 4 BCE).

Yet accuracy of this nature and at this level is probably not the best criterion by which to judge Luke or any historian. Almost certainly Luke was striving for accuracy at this level; and almost certainly he may not have achieved perfection. After all, if he were writing 30–40 years after the events of the Pauline mission, it is scarcely surprising that one or two details have been accidentally confused; and despite having excellent knowledge about some aspects of the Roman Empire (e.g. the politarchs in Thessalonica), he may have had a slightly less than perfect grasp of the relative chronology of people like Herod, Quirinius *et al*.

But that is perhaps not so important. Luke as a historian is not interested *just* in dates and places, the dry facts and nothing more. No historians worth their salt ever have been, and ancient historians are no exception. Ancient historians (like modern ones!) write not only to present facts but also to get across a message. A historian like Livy writes his history to commend his national cause and to present ideals for moral conduct through his characters. In the Old Testament, the deuteronomistic historian presents his account of Jewish history in such a way as to illustrate his theology that virtue is rewarded and sin punished by God in this worldly terms; the Chronicler in turn rewrites the deuteronomistic history to be even more deuteronomic than the Deuteronomists themselves: hence the stories are changed so that, for example, good kings who die young must have been bad, and bad kings who lived long must have been good. Thus Manasseh repents in 2 Chron. 33.12-13; Josiah, a good king who died young, disobeys in 2 Chron. 35.21. So too Josephus writes his histories to defend the status of the Jewish people in the eyes of non-Jewish detractors. All this suggests that if Luke is a historian, then he is doing far more than just trying to get his dates and places correct. He is writing with a purpose, and presenting his story to further that purpose. What then might that purpose be?

One possibility which has been very influential in the past has been that Luke is in part writing to counter worries about eschatological beliefs: in particular he is writing to apologize for the delay in the parousia. In the next chapter we shall therefore consider the question of Luke's eschatology.

Further Reading

L.C.A. Alexander, *The Preface to Luke's Gospel* (SNTSMS, 78; Cambridge: Cambridge University Press, 1993).

H.J. Cadbury, 'Commentary on the Preface of Luke', in F.J. Foakes Jackson and K. Lake (eds.), *The Beginnings of Christianity* (London: Macmillan, 1922), II, pp. 489-510.

D.R. Catchpole, *The Quest for Q* (Edinburgh: T. & T. Clark, 1993).

W.R. Farmer, *The Synoptic Problem* (Dillsboro' NC: Western North Carolina Press, repr. 1976 [1964]).

J.A. Fitzmyer, 'The Priority of Mark and the "Q" Source in Luke', in D.G. Miller (ed.), *Jesus and Man's Hope* (Pittsburgh: Pittsburgh Theological Seminary, 1970), I, pp. 131-70; repr. in *To Advance the Gospel* (New York: Crossroad, 1981), pp. 3-40.

M.D. Goulder, *Luke—A New Paradigm* (JSNTSup, 20; Sheffield: JSOT Press, 1989).

J.C. O'Neill, *The Theology of Acts in its Historical Setting* (London: SPCK, 1970).

B.H. Streeter, *The Four Gospels* (London: Macmillan, 1924).

V. Taylor, *Behind the Third Gospel* (London: Macmillan, 1926).

—*The Passion Narrative of St Luke* (SNTSMS, 19; Cambridge: Cambridge University Press, 1972).

C.M. Tuckett, 'Synoptic Problem', *ABD* (1992), pp. 263-70.
—'The Existence of Q', in R.A. Piper (ed.), *The Gospel behind the Gospels. Current Studies on Q* (NovTSup, 75; Leiden: Brill, 1995), pp. 19-47.

2

ESCHATOLOGY

ONE OF THE CLASSIC STUDIES of Luke's redactional activity was that of H. Conzelmann's 1953 book *Die Mitte der Zeit* (*The Middle of Time*), translated into English with the blander title *The Theology of St Luke*. A key part of Conzelmann's discussion concerned Luke's eschatology, and ever since, eschatology has been regarded as a key area in any study of Luke's concerns.

Conzelmann's basic theory is that Luke's church was faced with a crisis at the end of the first century, due to the fact that the parousia, the return of Jesus in glory and the end of the present world order, had failed to materialize as predicted. Faced with this situation, Luke undertook a radical revision of his Christian tradition to eliminate expectation of an imminent End from his sources. Thus for Luke, the parousia was no longer to be expected soon, but only at the end of an almost indefinite future. And in place of the stock early Christian belief in eschatology, Luke substituted a belief in *Heilsgeschichte*, salvation history. In this the history of the world was seen as the sphere of God's saving activity, through the ministry of Jesus, and in the life of the church, which would carry on for a considerable time as far as Luke was concerned. In this scheme, salvation history was conceived of as divided into three clear, mutually exclusive epochs: the era of the Old Testament which reached up to and including John the Baptist (Lk. 16.16 is often appealed to by Conzelmann in this context), the era of Jesus (the 'middle of time' of Conzelmann's original title) which Conzelmann thought was free from influence of Satan (cf. Lk. 4.13; 22.3) and the era of the church. In this too the history of the church was no longer regarded as eschatological in any sense, and the gift of the Holy Spirit to the church was no longer regarded as the eschatological gift, but rather as a substitute for the Eschaton.

Such, in very brief outline, is Conzelmann's theory about eschatology in Luke. The theory has been enormously influential, convincing many and provoking others to criticize in detail parts or all of the total schema. We should, however, note that the schema is a very complex one with many aspects, some of which do tend to become rather jumbled in the discussion if one is not careful.

Salvation History

It is probably fully justified to say that Luke has a strong and powerful idea of salvation history. We have already seen that Luke probably wishes to present his work self-consciously as that of a historian, that is, he writes a history. Luke alone of the evangelists takes care to situate the story he relates into the wider context of world history (cf. the attempted synchronization with broader world history in Lk. 2.1; 3.1, despite the problems of detailed accuracy which these verses engender), and it is clearly important for him that Paul can say to Festus of the life and history of the church: 'These things were not done in a corner' (Acts 26.26). Further, this history is one in which Luke believes God is active, and acting purposefully, to bring salvation to humankind. The idea that the whole of history is under the control and guidance of God is reflected in a number of references throughout Luke–Acts to God's plan (Lk. 7.30; Acts 2.23; 4.28; 5.38-39; 13.26; 20.27), or will (Lk. 22.42; Acts 21.14), as well as references to the necessity of what is happening (the Greek word *dei*, 'it is necessary', is used 18 times in Luke, 24 times in Acts: cf. Lk. 2.49; 4.43; 9.22; 13.33 etc.), and the foreknowledge and predetermination of God in planning all that happens (perhaps more common in Acts: cf. Acts 2.23; 3.20; 4.28; 10.41 etc., but also Lk. 22.22). (For the whole theme, see Squires 1993.)

So too Luke, perhaps more than other New Testament writers, shows a greater awareness that the events of Jesus lie in the *past*. For writers like Mark and Paul, a case can be made that they have to some extent collapsed the time between past and present (though of course not entirely!). Thus for Mark, the gospel of Jesus and preached by Jesus (Mk 1.1; 1.14) is also the present gospel for which Christians suffer, which is so closely parallel to Jesus (Mk 8.35; 10.29) that there is almost a sense in which Jesus is present in the Gospel and the two come together. For Paul, the 'day of salvation' is the 'now' of Paul's own preaching and proclamation (2 Cor. 6.2, a verse often adduced to compare with Luke's view). By contrast, the 'now' of salvation for Luke is the *past* event of Jesus in the synagogue in Nazareth (Lk. 4.21: '*today* this Scripture has been fulfilled in your hearing').

However, it would probably be quite wrong to drive too much of a wedge between Luke and other early Christian writers in this respect. Paul almost certainly has just as much of an idea of God being active in history, and hence salvation history in this sense, as Luke does (cf. Rom. 4; 9–11; 1 Cor. 10.1-11; Gal. 4.4-6); and it is very unlikely that Mark has abolished the distinction between the ministry of Jesus in the past and his own present preaching of the Gospel entirely.

Conzelmann's detailed theory of a very specific threefold schema of salvation history has been much discussed and much criticized: for example it is not at all clear that John the Baptist belongs to the old era of the Old Testament and not to the new Christian dispensation for Luke; the description of Jesus' ministry as 'Satan free' is questionable (cf. Lk. 10.18; 11.14-20; 13.16); and it is often unclear in Conzelmann's theory exactly where the dividing line between the epoch of Jesus and that of the church lies: is it at 22.3 with the arrival on Satan on the scene? Or at 22.36 where Jesus apparently rescinds the previous instructions about money and possessions? Or at Jesus' death? Or at the ascension? Or at Pentecost?

However, these criticisms do not necessarily affect the basic schema. John the Baptist could quite happily be shifted from the Old Testament era to the era of Jesus (and probably should be) without altering the underlying theory significantly. So too, despite some ambiguity and unclarity about the precise dividing line between the era of Jesus and the era of the church, there are clear differences between the two. For example, the most obvious is that Jesus is present in his ministry, but mainly absent in the era of the church: the ascension serves in Luke to remove Jesus from the sphere of activity of Christians, and the prime medium of God's saving activity is now the Holy Spirit, who/which in turn has been mostly—and remarkably—absent during the time of the ministry of Jesus himself.

(It is one of the peculiar features of Luke's Gospel that Luke seems to want to generate an enormous expectation of activity by the Spirit in the ministry of Jesus in the first four chapters of the Gospel, but then this never seems to materialize. The birth narratives witness to a great upsurge of activity by the Spirit in prophetic outbursts by various figures. Jesus himself is baptized with the Spirit in ch. 3, led by the Spirit into the desert for the temptations in ch. 4, and then, in a scene in which Luke clearly invests an enormous amount of narrative significance, announces that the prophecy of Isaiah of being anointed by the Spirit has been fulfilled in himself [4.16–21]. Yet after this, the Spirit is barely mentioned in relation to Jesus' activity. Rather, the sphere of the Spirit's activity seems to be that of 'the church in the period *after* Jesus has departed. Why Luke is so silent about any activity of the Spirit in Jesus' ministry after ch. 4 is something of an enigma.)

Overall then, despite possible differences of opinion in some details, it seems clear that Luke does work with an idea of salvation history. Moreover, there is also some idea of significantly different periods in this history, although the dividing lines may be placed in a slightly different way than Conzelmann suggested, and the lines themselves may be at times slightly blurred. Whether we should think of a *three*fold division as the governing one in Luke's schema will be considered shortly.

Delay of the Parousia?

Did Luke believe that the parousia had been delayed? And did he then radically rewrite his sources in the light of this to eradicate such an expectation entirely? The two questions are in fact rather different and should probably be separated. As we shall see shortly, Luke is probably aware of a delay in the Parousia. However, to claim that this was due to a crisis which only hit the church in Luke's day would go beyond the evidence. It may of course be that Luke's community had never bothered about the non-appearance of the parousia until Luke's day. But this seems unlikely. Certainly we know of other Christians in the first century adjusting in various ways to the fact that history was going on without interruption. For example, Paul, writing perhaps 30–40 years before Luke, seems to have moved from a position of expecting the parousia in his own lifetime (1 Thess. 4.15; 1 Cor. 15.51) to a position where he seems to anticipate that he will himself die before any parousia event (Phil. 1.23; perhaps 2 Cor. 5.2-4). So too Mark's apocalyptic chapter in Mark 13 probably shows some awareness that history has gone on rather longer than some at least were anticipating. In any case, any problems of a delay in the parousia would presumably have arisen well before the 80s or 90s of the first century. By this stage almost all the first generation of Christians and contemporaries of Jesus must have died. It is hardly likely then that Luke was the first to face any problem caused by the delay of the parousia.

Nevertheless, even if Luke may not have been unique, and Christians had faced the problem of the delay of the parousia before Luke's day, this does not mean that Luke was *not* concerned with this issue! There is certainly quite a lot of evidence to suggest that Luke was aware of the delay of the parousia and he adjusted some his traditions accordingly. This can be seen in a number of places.

Awareness of Delay

The most famous example is Luke's rewriting of Mk 14.62 in Lk. 22.69. Here, in the reply of Jesus to the High Priest at the Sanhedrin trial, Mark has Jesus predict 'You will see the Son of Man seated at the right hand of the Power, and coming with the clouds of heaven'. Luke has instead simply 'From now on the Son of Man will be seated at the right hand of the power of God'. By omitting the words 'coming with the clouds of heaven', and replacing 'you will see' by 'from now on', Luke has changed a prediction of a universally visible coming (presumably to earth) by Jesus as Son of Man to a statement about his position (presumably in heaven) which will take place immediately. Thus a prediction of a future parousia has been replaced by a statement about Jesus' present status (present, that is, for the author and the reader). It may be that embarrassment about the failure of the parousia to materialize has led to the change being made.

A similar concern may lie behind the introduction which Luke (and Luke alone) gives to his version of the parable of the pounds in Lk. 19.11: here Luke says that Jesus told this parable to the disciples 'because he was near Jerusalem and they thought that the kingdom of God was about to appear immediately'. The parable of the man going away and entrusting his servants with money seems to have been interpreted in terms of Jesus' going away and returning at the parousia with the explicit warning that any return is not going to take place immediately. It looks then as if Luke is aware that Jesus' return has been delayed.

It is possible (though not certain) that the same concern lies behind Luke's apparent change to Mk 9.1 in Lk. 9.27. In Mark, Jesus predicts that 'There are some standing here who will not taste death until they see the kingdom of God come with power'. Luke, in reproducing this verse, omits the final words 'come with power'. In Mark the prediction is clearly of a cosmic event to take place in the lifetime of the audience. In Luke the saying is at least open to a rather different interpretation: the 'kingdom' might be more of a spiritual reality, or the 'seeing' might be not related to quite such a visual event. However, the precise interpretation of Luke's version here is much disputed.

The initial summary of Jesus' preaching in Mark is 'The kingdom of God has come near' (Mk 1.15). Luke replaces this initial summary with his grand scene of the rejection of Jesus at Nazareth (Lk. 4.16-30), and the summary statement of Jesus' message is no longer about the imminence of the kingdom, but the claim that Scripture has now been fulfilled in the 'today' of Jesus' presence (Lk. 4.21).

An awareness of some delay in the parousia seems to be evident in a number of other small changes Luke makes to

Mark, especially in the apocalyptic discourse of Mark 13, which Luke rewrites in Luke 21. For example, in Lk. 21.8, Luke adds to Mark a warning of what false claimants might say. In Mark they will come and make some claim by saying 'I am he!' (Mk 13.5: the precise interpretation of this is disputed); Luke adds to this a warning about people who will say 'The time is near!' Warnings of an imminent End seem to be rejected by Luke's Jesus as those of false claimants.

We have already noted in another context that Luke rewrites the apocalyptic and enigmatic language of Mk 13.14, which refers to the desolating sacrilege, by making a clear allusion to the fall of Jerusalem: 'When you see Jerusalem surrounded by armies' (Lk. 21.20). It looks as if Luke then has interpreted the enigmatic Markan verse as a clear reference to the fall of Jerusalem which for Luke is now past and hence *not* a prelude to the End.

In line with this too, Luke makes a small change to the beginning of the paragraph containing this verse. In Mk 13.9 Mark has Jesus predict persecution for the disciples which appears to follow the wars and earthquakes and famines of Mk 13.8. Luke adds here 'But before all this occurs...' (Lk. 21.12), so that the persecution etc. of the disciples is predicted to take place before the natural disasters etc. Perhaps then again Luke knows that persecutions have taken place and have not heralded the End.

Above all we should note here what is a remarkable silence in Acts about the any idea of an imminent End. At the start of Acts, the disciples ask the risen Jesus whether he is going to restore the kingdom to Israel 'at this time' (Acts 1.6). Jesus brushes aside the question, telling them 'it is not for you to know the times or periods that the Father has set by his own authority' (1.7). Thus any temporal concerns about the End are swept away and the disciples are told to go and be witnesses 'in Jerusalem, in all Judea and Samaria, and to the ends of the earth' (1.8). Thereafter, there is hardly any reference to an imminent End event in the preaching of the church's mission. Occasionally it is referred to in general terms (Acts 3.21; 10.42; 17.31), but with no indication that such an event might be imminent.

Individual Eschatology?

There is a further small body of evidence in Luke–Acts which may be relevant here. This concerns a few verses which may suggest that Luke had moved away from the view, wide-spread as far as we can tell in early Christianity, whereby men and women expected a great irruption into the world which would bring about the end of the present world order and the final judgment of humankind; instead Luke may have adopted a more 'individual eschatology', whereby the decisive moment of judgment took place at each individual's death.

In support of this one can refer to the parable of the Rich Man and Lazarus (Lk. 16.19-31), where both parties seem to receive their final reward or punishment immediately after death. So too Jesus' words to the dying thief on the cross, 'Today you will be with me in Paradise' (Lk. 23.43) may point in the same way. Similar too is the account of the death of Stephen who says that he sees the Son of Man standing (Acts 7.56), language which is more normally associated with the parousia and the final judgment at the end of time (cf. Lk. 12.8 etc.), and perhaps then indicating an individualized parousia for Stephen at the time of his own physical death.

The evidence is not entirely clear and it is uncertain precisely how it should be interpreted. The evidence is certainly not extensive, and in any case could be interpreted along slightly different lines, for example, the position of individuals who have just died could be thought of as in some kind of intermediate waiting stage, prior to final judgment itself. (Such an idea can be well attested in Jewish thought of the time.) Perhaps it may show too that Luke is not entirely consistent in his thinking.

The net result of all the evidence considered so far, whether about the delay of the parousia or about the possible reinterpretation of eschatological hopes in an individualized direction, has suggested to many that Luke is conscious of the delay in the parousia and has adjusted his source material in quite a major way to reflect that concern. The trouble is that there is a significant amount of evidence in Luke's Gospel that gives a very different picture, suggesting that an imminent End should be taken very seriously. We need therefore to glance briefly at this evidence.

Imminent End?

In Lk. 3.9, Luke repeats (from Q) the preaching of John the Baptist, warning of an imminent destructive power: 'Even now the axe is lying at the root of the trees'. In Luke's account of the mission of the 70, the 70 are told to greet both receptive and unreceptive cities with the greeting/warning 'the kingdom of God has come near' (Lk. 10.9, 11). (The first of these may be from Q: cf. Mt. 10.7; the second has no parallel in Matthew and hence may be Luke's own addition to what is basically Q material.) The parables of the thief at night and the waiting servants (Lk. 12.39-40, 42-46) both warn of an event which may come at any moment and catch out those who are unprepared with disastrous consequences. The same message comes out in the apocalyptic material Luke takes from Q in Lk. 17.23-37: for example, vv. 26-30 have Jesus warn that the day of the Son of Man will catch people unawares just as the flood in the days of Noah, or the fire and brimstone in the days of Lot. So too, at the end of the parable of the widow and the unjust judge in Lk. 18.1-8, Luke's Jesus claims that God will vindicate his elect 'quickly'.

Finally, Luke retains from Mark 13 the clear statement that everything predicted in the preceding discourse will happen before 'this generation' passes away (Lk. 21.32, cf. Mk 13.30). It is true that there is a slight change in that Luke omits the word for 'these' in Mark, so that in Luke Jesus says that this generation will not pass away until 'all things', rather than 'all these things', happen. However, it is difficult to see how this really affects the problem in relation to the prediction of an end of the world within the lifetime of the present generation. There have been attempts too to reinterpret the word for 'generation' here, as if it might refer to the whole human race (cf. commentaries on this verse); but this does not seem entirely convincing.

There is then a substantial body of material in Luke's Gospel which seems to be not the slightest bit embarrassed about affirming a hope of an eschatological climax which is about to come, and warning of the dire consequences which will fall on those who are not prepared.

How then can one resolve this apparent tension? On the

one hand Luke seems to be at pains to play down predictions by Jesus of an imminent End; on the other, he has elements which vigorously and positively urge such a belief.

Possible Solutions

A number of possible solutions have been proposed. Conzelmann, who argued that Luke's dominant concern was to apologize for the delay in the parousia, claimed that the elements in Luke stressing an imminent End were simply vestiges from Luke's sources. For example, John the Baptist's warning in Lk. 3.9, the parables in Luke 12 and the eschatological warnings in Luke 17 are all from Q; the saying about this generation not passing away before everything happens is from Mark. This is, however, not very satisfactory. As we saw when considering the proper method of redaction criticism, we cannot ignore material which a writer has taken from a source without altering it. Such material is potentially just as significant for determining an author's concerns as any positive changes to a source which can be identified (see p. 26 above). Hence we have to take seriously the fact of both strands in Luke.

Some have suggested that Luke may have been faced with a dual situation in his community, and the two strands of Luke's eschatology meet each half of this dual situation: in the face of a delay in the parousia, some may have given up hope altogether—hence the stress on the imminence; others may have developed a fanatical belief that the End was very near, and even already present—and hence Luke stresses the delay motif (see Wilson 1973).

Again this is not entirely convincing. The duality in the situation is never explicit, and such a theory makes for a somewhat schizoid community; presumably too the situation would be open to some abuse since, if each party in the community read the wrong bit of the Gospel, they would be confirmed in their (for Luke) dangerous views, rather than being corrected; and there is no indication that the Gospel is to be read selectively by different people.

No solution is entirely satisfactory, but perhaps the one that explains most of the evidence is related to the view we have already referred to that Luke is a historian. Luke is conscious of the fact that the events of Jesus' life and death are now past. He is also aware of the delay in the parousia, at least insofar as quite a lot of water has flowed under the metaphorical bridge since Jesus' day and the parousia has not materialized. In this sense Conzelmann is right: Luke is concerned about the delay of the parousia. But Luke may *not* have yet given up the hope and expectation of the End for his own day. Thus Conzelmann may be wrong to suggest that Luke has postponed the parousia into the indefinite future. Rather, Luke may still want to reaffirm the eschatological hope in his own time and hence preserves some of the elements in his tradition which warn of a sudden End that may arrive at any moment. Thus for Luke, Jesus predicts delay, and Luke tones down some of the predictions of the parousia that Jesus makes; but this is not because Luke himself has surrendered all such hope completely. Rather it may be precisely in order to reaffirm such hope in his own day that Luke rewrites his sources in this way (see Hiers 1974; Carroll 1988).

In due course, Christians did have to make considerable adjustments to their eschatological timetables and beliefs. The parousia did not happen as expected, and Christians eventually had to come to terms with the fact that the era of the church was going to last for some considerable time. Within the New Testament, such an adjustment may already have taken place with the writer of Ephesians (probably not Paul) who evidently thinks of the church as the place where God's glory is displayed 'to all generations, forever and ever' (Eph. 3.21). But it seems unlikely that Luke himself had yet taken that step.

Significance of the Present

A final plank of Conzelmann's overall theory was that Luke attributed little eschatological significance to the present: the Eschaton had shifted to the distant future, and the gift of the Spirit to the church in the present was just a substitute for the Eschaton.

This is, however, not fully persuasive. Indeed it may be shown to be misleading by some of the evidence we have considered already. The most famous example of Luke's alleged concern to apologize for the delay of the parousia is often held to be his rewriting of Mk 14.62 in Lk. 22.69 (see above). However, we also need to bear in mind not only what Luke does not say (by omitting or changing elements from Mark), but also what he does say. As noted already in general terms, no reader of Luke's present text without the benefit of a Synopsis (or perhaps very detailed knowledge of Mark's text) would pick up that this is apologizing for a delay in the parousia. Rather, what the verse is doing is stressing the immense significance and importance of Jesus' *present* position (i.e. present for Luke): Jesus is now at God's right hand in glory and that is what is of paramount concern for Luke. In Luke's story, Jesus takes his place in this position by virtue of his ascension, and it is the ascension of Jesus to the position of glory that all scholars agree is of central significance for Luke (cf. especially Franklin 1975).

But for Luke the importance of the present applies not only to the situation in the post-ascension era. For Luke it is of central significance that the whole era of Jesus and the church is one of the *fulfilment* of Jewish hopes and expectations. To this we now turn.

Prophecy and Fulfilment

As far as the era of the church is concerned, this is perhaps clearest in the Pentecost story of Acts 2. Here, in Acts 2.17-21, the gift of the Spirit is explicitly portrayed as the fulfilment of the prophecy of the Old Testament in Joel 2.23-27 (LXX 3.1-5). Further, it is significant that Luke almost certainly alters the text of the LXX of Joel from 'after these things' to 'in the last days' (v. 17). (This reading in Acts 2.17 is, however, slightly uncertain in view of a textual variant in a few manuscripts of Acts which read 'after these things', agreeing with the LXX. This may well be due to assimilation to the LXX and hence is probably not original.) Luke's version (which actually now agrees with the Hebrew text of Joel 2) indicates clearly (pace Conzelmann) that the gift of the Spirit is not a replacement or a substitute for the Eschaton. Rather, the presence of the Spirit implies the *fulfilment* of eschatological hopes and indicates that the last days have in a real sense already arrived. Far from pushing the Eschaton into the indefinite future, Luke brings it firmly into the present.

This note of fulfilment, especially the fulfilment of Scripture, runs through many parts of Luke–Acts. We shall leave aside any detailed discussion of Acts, though we may note in passing the way in which key events in the story in Acts are presented as fulfilling Scripture: for example, Judas's defection fulfils Ps. 69.26 (Acts 1.20); the Gentile mission is said by James in Acts 15.16-17 to be in fulfilment of the Scripture of Amos 9.11-12 (though 'James' needs the LXX of Amos to show this!), and the final rejection (if that is what it is) by Paul of the Jews in Rome is portrayed as the fulfilment of Isa. 6.9-10 in Acts 28.26-27.

Such a note of prophetic fulfilment—explicitly of scripture, or more generally—is a prominent feature of Luke's Gospel as well. We have already noted the importance of the inaugural scene in Nazareth in Luke's narrative (Lk. 4.16-30), with the focal point of Jesus' speech in his claim that 'Today this Scripture [Isa. 61.1-12] has been fulfilled in your hearing' (v. 21). Such explicit references to a specific proof text are perhaps less common in Luke, and more characteristic of Matthew in the Gospels. But Luke has no less firm an idea than Matthew that the Gospel events fulfil scripture, even if the picture is sometimes painted with broader strokes of the brush.

Luke is, for example, convinced that Jesus' sufferings and death are in fulfilment of Scripture (though he rarely says which particular texts he has in mind). This is of course explicit in relation to the specific text of Isaiah 53 in the story of the Ethiopian eunuch in Acts 8. But in more general terms, Luke rewrites Mark's third passion prediction in Mk 10.33 completely, changing Mark's 'The Son of Man will be handed over to the chief priests and the scribes' to read instead 'Everything that is written about the Son of Man by the prophets will be accomplished' (Lk. 18.31). Thus the whole of the passion is brought under the rubric of Scripture fulfilled.

This comes out very strongly indeed in the scenes Luke records of the teaching given by the risen Jesus to the disciples at the end of the Gospel in Luke 24. Here Jesus tells the disciples on the road to Emmaus that everything that has happened to him, including his passion, was foretold in Scripture (Lk. 24.26-27), a claim that is then repeated when Jesus meets the eleven in the upper room (Lk. 24.44-46). Similarly Luke has characters in Acts say three times that the suffering of the Messiah is foretold in Scripture (Acts 3.18; 17.3; 26.22-23).

The same general idea of the time of Jesus as the era of fulfilment is provided by the birth narratives. As already indicated (p. 24 above), these are probably no afterthought, added as an optional extra to the rest of the story. Rather, they incorporate many key Lukan themes. Here we may note simply the way in which they portray in general terms the outburst of prophetic activity and the work of the Spirit. As we have already seen, the Spirit for Luke (as indeed for many parts of Judaism) was thought of as the gift of the End-time. The sudden outburst of activity of the Spirit, as portrayed in Luke's account of the birth narratives, is there-fore extremely significant. Not only is the Holy Spirit the power which engenders the birth of Jesus himself (Lk. 1.35), the Spirit also inspires a series of individuals in various ways. Thus it is predicted that John the Baptist will be 'filled with the Holy Spirit' (1.15), Elizabeth is filled with the Spirit to sing her praise of Mary (1.41); perhaps there is too a hint of the activity of the Spirit in Mary's own song of praise, the Magnificat (1.47: 'My spirit rejoices in God my Saviour'). Zachariah is filled with the Spirit as he utters the Benedictus (1.67), just as the Spirit 'rested on' Simeon as he comes to the temple (2.25) to utter the Nunc Dimittis (2.29-32). This outburst of prophetic activity by the Spirit thus clearly marks the era of Jesus as one of eschatological fulfilment of Jewish hopes.

The same may also be indicated by one of the words in Luke's prologue. In Lk. 1.1 Luke refers to the events he is going to cover in his work as 'the events that have been ful-filled among us' (NRSV). The verb translated here 'fulfilled' is in Greek *peplērophorēmenōn*. Its precise meaning is a little uncertain, and it may simply be a rather flowery way of saying 'the events that have happened'. However the Greek root *plēro-*, from which this verb comes, is a highly significant one for Christian terminology referring to the 'fulfilment' which is claimed for the Christ-event. It is therefore quite likely that Luke has this deeper meaning in mind so that the events he is about to describe have not merely 'happened' in his view, but have happened by way of 'fulfilling' ancient hopes and expectations. (On this general theme, see Dahl 1966; Schubert 1954; Tiede 1980.)

Salvation

Perhaps relevant too is the stress Luke places on the 'salvation' which is now available through the preaching of Jesus and the missionary activity of the early church. Luke is famous for using the vocabulary of 'salvation', or being 'saved', and speaking of Jesus as 'Saviour', more frequently than other New Testament writers. It is part of Luke's characteristic vocabulary to describe the benefits which the Christian gospel brings to men and women.

Yet for the New Testament generally, 'salvation' is an eschatological gift. For example, salvation for Paul is entirely future and the part of the eschatological blessings which has yet to come (cf. Rom. 5.9-10). For Luke it is implied that it is available in the present. Jesus himself is the 'Saviour' (Lk. 2.11), and 'salvation' is announced by Zachariah in the Benedictus (Lk. 1.71, 77). Zacchaeus is told by Jesus, when he responds positively, that 'Today *salvation* has come to this house' (Lk. 19.9). The sinful woman in Luke 7 and the leper who returns to Jesus to thank him are both told 'your faith has *saved* you' (Lk. 7.50; 17.19), and Jesus summarizes his work by saying that 'the Son of Man came to seek out and to *save* the lost' (Lk. 19.10). So too in Acts the 'salvation' available in Jesus, and in Jesus alone, is a strong motif in the church's preaching (Acts 4.12; 13.26, 47; 16.17).

It is, of course, not absolutely certain that Luke was aware of such eschatological significance in the word, but it seems not improbable that in his stress on the 'salvation' that is available in the Christian message, Luke is again stressing the present as the era of the fulfilment of old hopes and expectations.

Conclusion

We have looked at various aspects of Luke's eschatology in this chapter, especially in the light of Conzelmann's work on Luke–Acts which has done so much to shape contemporary Lukan scholarship. I have tried to argue that while some aspects of his overall theory are valid, other parts may perhaps need modification. Luke does write with an idea of salvation history; and there is a real sense in which he has a threefold division of such history in mind. But there is a deeper sense in which perhaps this threefold division is better seen as a twofold division. Despite real differences between the time of Jesus and the time of the church (cf. p. 36 above), both are together the era of fulfilment of the prophetic hopes and expectations of Judaism. Moreover, rather than postponing the Eschaton into the indefinite future, Luke still has a firm hope for an imminent eschatological event, while at the same time affirming a belief in the present as in a very real sense a realization of some of these eschatological events (e.g. the activity of the Holy Spirit).

Yet this raises a serious question. If the events of Jesus and the Christian church fulfil Jewish Scripture, why have the Jews themselves not responded positively? Luke–Acts is famous for showing how the Christian gospel has gone to the Gentiles. Indeed Luke's Gospel is sometimes known as the Gospel for the Gentiles; and Luke's story ends in Acts with Paul uttering what have appeared to many as words expressing a final and definitive rejection of the Jewish people (Acts 28.26-27, citing Isa. 6.9-10). What then is Luke's attitude to the Jewish people and/or Judaism? This will be the topic of the next chapter.

Further Reading

J.T. Carroll, *Responses to the End of History. Eschatology and Situation in Luke–Acts* (SBLDS, 92; Atlanta: Scholars Press, 1988).

H. Conzelmann, *The Theology of Saint Luke* (ET; London: Faber, 1960).

N.A. Dahl, 'The Story of Abraham in Luke–Acts', in Keck & Martin (eds.), *Studies in Luke–Acts*, pp. 139–58.

R.H. Hiers, 'The Problem of the Delay in the Parousia in Luke–Acts', *NTS* 20 (1974) pp. 145-55.

R. Maddox, *The Purpose of Luke–Acts* (Edinburgh: T. & T. Clark, 1982), esp. ch. 5, 'The Lucan Eschatology', pp. 100–57.

P. Schubert, 'The Structure and Significance of Luke 24', in W. Eltester (ed.), *Neutestamentliche Studien für Rudolf Bultmann* (Berlin: Töpelmann, 1954), pp. 165–86.

J.T. Squires, *The Plan of God in Luke–Acts* (SNTSMS, 76; Cambridge: Cambridge University Press, 1993).

D.L. Tiede, *Prophecy and History in Luke–Acts* (Philadelphia: Fortress Press, 1980).

S.G. Wilson, *The Gentiles and the Gentile Mission in Luke–Acts* (SNTSMS, 23; Cambridge: Cambridge University Press, 1973), esp. ch. 3, 'Lukan Eschatology', pp. 59–87 (= *NTS* 16 [1970], pp. 330-47).

3

JEWS, GENTILES AND JUDAISM

THE SUBJECT OF LUKE'S ATTITUDE to Jews and/or Judaism is perhaps one of the most controversial in contemporary Lukan studies. That the question is an important one for Luke is scarcely to be doubted; and of course the whole issue is given added significance for all who have to live and work as biblical exegetes in a post-Holocaust era. There is no doubt that some parts of the New Testament can be read in a way that some describe as anti-Semitic. Luke's writings are no exception in this regard, and hence this aspect of Luke's work has increasingly come under critical scrutiny in recent years. Two preliminary points should be made first.

(i) In one way it might be thought that the whole topic is more to do with the interpretation of Acts, rather than of Luke's Gospel. It is certainly true that a great deal of the relevant evidence comes from Acts. But we cannot say that the issue has no relevance for the interpretation of the Gospel as well. Key parts of the Gospel, including the birth narratives, the rejection scene in Nazareth (Lk. 4.16-30), the passion narrative, as well as the denunciations of the Jewish audience in the Gospel, are all clearly also relevant, and their interpretation depends significantly on the overall interpretation one adopts in relation to this wider issue. In any case, I have already tried to show that, in general terms, one cannot interpret Luke's Gospel in isolation from Acts. Thus, although the prime focus of this book is Luke's Gospel, we shall have to take the evidence from Acts fully into account here.

(ii) The interpretation of the evidence is also crucially connected with one's understanding of more so-called introductory problems of who Luke was, who he was writing for, and why he was writing. Further, it is really impossible to separate these issues from the broader questions of Luke's atttude to Judaism. As we shall see, one's decisions on the latter question may not only be informed by, but also to a certain extent determine, one's answers to the more introductory questions. At the very least there is an inevitable element of circularity here.

The whole question is, as I said, a controversial one in current Lukan studies. This is due in no small measure to the fact that the evidence in Luke seems to point in different ways simultaneously. This has led one recent writer to say that 'Luke–Acts is one of the most pro-Jewish and one of the most anti-Jewish writings in the New Testament' (Gaston 1986: 153). But perhaps before we consider Luke and Judaism, we should consider Luke's attitude to Gentiles.

Gentiles

Traditionally Luke has been considered the most pro-Gentile of all the evangelists. Above all, the evidence of Acts, and the account of the success of the Gentile mission there, is often adduced. Thus many have taken the command in Acts 1.8 by the risen Jesus to the disciples, that they are to be 'witnesses in Jerusalem, in all Judea and Samaria, and to the ends of the earth', as a programmatic summary of the book of Acts itself, which shows how the gospel does spread out from Jerusalem and Judea (chs. 1–7) to Samaria (ch. 8) and on to the ends of the world (symbolically represented by Rome) in the ensuing spread of the Gentile mission (chs. 9–28). Whether this is an appropriate interpretation of Acts we shall leave on one side here, but it is clearly a matter of considerable importance of Acts to show the spread of the mission to reach beyond the national boundaries of Judaism.

When we turn to Luke's Gospel, it is perhaps surprising that there is relatively little to do with this theme. It is certainly true that there are hints of what is to come, but these are mostly by way of a preview of the future. Thus Simeon in the temple says of the infant Jesus that he will be 'a light to lighten the Gentiles', and provide 'salvation which you have prepared in the presence of all peoples' (Lk. 2.32, 31). In the introduction to the preaching of John the Baptist, Luke takes over from Mark the citation of Isa. 40.3 ('a voice crying in the wilderness...'), but extends it as far as Isa. 40.5, to include the words 'All flesh shall see the salvation of God' (Lk. 3.5), showing not only Luke's interest in the vocabulary of salvation, but also his concern to bring out the universal nature of that salvation.

In the rejection scene in Nazareth (Lk. 4.16-30), Luke's Jesus refers to the examples of Elijah and Elisha as prophets sent to those *out*side their own *patris* (Lk. 4.25-27), to illustrate the claim that 'no prophet is accepted in his own *patris*' (v. 24). It is clear in the context that the Greek word *patris* in v. 23 means home *town* ('Whatever we have heard done in Capernaum, do here in your own *patris*'); but in v. 24 may shift its meaning to become home *country*, and is illustrated by the stories of Elijah and Elisha going outside the limits of Israel (to the widow of Zarephthah and Naaman the Syrian respectively). Thus the story as a whole, which is widely regarded as a programmatic summary of the whole of Luke's story to come, probably here points forward to the way in which the gospel will be taken to non-Jews.

In the ministry of Jesus itself as recorded in the Gospel, there is, however, little on this directly. Unlike the Jesus of the other Gospels, Luke's Jesus does not really have any direct contact with a Gentile. The story of Jesus and the Syro-Phoenician woman in Mk. 7.24-30 is part of a whole section of Mark (6.45–8.26) omitted by Luke. The reasons for this omission are not entirely clear. In part it may be because the material is somewhat repetitive (e.g. the feeding of the 4000 after the feeding of the 5000), in part because some parts may have been felt to be offensive (e.g. the stories in Mk 7.32-37; 8.22-26, where Jesus uses what could have been regarded as magical techniques), but also in part because Luke knew that Jesus did not go into Gentile territory (as Mark records him doing in this section). Alternatively, Luke may have wished to avoid such an impression quite deliberately, because in his somewhat schematic version of history, the Gospel only goes to the Gentiles in the era of the church under the guidance of the Spirit and (to a certain extent) only when the Jews have rejected its offer.

As part of the same phenomenon, it may be quite deliberate on Luke's part that the healing of the centurion's servant in Lk. 7.1-10 takes place without the centurion ever meeting Jesus (unlike Matthew, Luke has the centurion send messengers to Jesus, and Luke may have added this detail himself, precisely in order to keep any contact between Jesus and Gentiles as at most indirect.)

Luke duplicates the story of the mission of the disciples, so that alongside a mission of the 12 (Lk. 9.1-6) there is a mission of the 70 (Lk. 10.1-16). It is possible that the latter prefigures the Gentile mission, with the number 70 perhaps intended to correspond to the total number of the nations of the world. However, this is at best implicit, and the story itself in Luke 10 does not indicate that the 70 themselves visit Gentiles.

In the parable of the Great Supper (Lk. 14.16-24), Luke seems to have expanded the end of the story so that the servants, who are sent out to find replacement guests for those who refused to come originally, cannot fill all the places at the first attempt and are sent out again. This detail (which is possibly superfluous in the parable as it stands) is lacking in Matthew's version of the parable, and may well be Luke's own addition to the story, the double mission of the servants now prefiguring the dual mission of the later church, to Jews and then to Gentiles.

Finally (at least in the Gospel's terms), in Lk. 24.47 the risen Jesus makes explicit what has so far been only adumbrated: the disciples are to go out in Jesus' name and proclaim repentance and the forgiveness of sins 'to all the nations, beginning from Jerusalem'. And this command is then taken up again at the beginning of Acts with the charge of the risen Jesus in Acts 1.8, which then leads on to the development of the story in the rest of Acts, as we have seen.

We may therefore say that the theme of the Gentiles' reception of the Gospel is an important one for Luke. It is, however, one which shows Luke's sensitivity as a historian. He is either aware of the fact that, or wants positively to

maintain that, Jesus himself did not have any extensive con-
tacts with Gentiles. For Luke then the Gentile mission is
prefigured in the Gospel; but it is not written back into the
pre-Easter story. Luke is conscious of the distinctions
between the different eras of history.

Jews and Judaism

What then of the other side of the coin? What is Luke's attitude to Jews and/or 'Judaism'? It is here that enormous
debate arises, in part simply because there is so much con-
flicting evidence. For on the one hand, there are elements of
Luke–Acts that seem extremely positive about Jews and
Judaism; on the other hand, there are elements that seem to
betray an intense, almost unrelieved, hostility.

As already noted, much of the relevant evidence is from
Acts; but, as I have said, we cannot ignore Acts if we wish to
come to some assessment of Luke's own attitudes and
concerns. In what follows I shall therefore allude to the Acts
evidence, but, as this is meant to be a study of Luke's Gospel,
not in such detail as if this were a study of the whole of the
Lukan writings equally. I consider the negative elements
first.

Anti-Judaism?

The negative attitude to Jews and Judaism does not dominate Luke's Gospel in a way that is necessarily qualitatively
different from the other Gospels, and such an attitude comes
much more to the fore in Acts. Nevertheless it is not lacking
in the Gospel.

The rejection scene in Nazareth (Lk. 4.16-30) acts, as we
have already noted, as a programmatic summary of the
whole story that is to follow in Luke's two-volume work, and
here the motif of the rejection of Jesus by the Jews is
sounded clearly. Further, if, as I argued above, the references
to Elijah and Elisha are rightly to be interpreted as
prefiguring the Gentile mission, then the division here
portrayed is clearly set in national or ethnic terms right from
the start.

In the rest of the Gospel, Luke preserves many of the
polemical, and at times extremely bitter, tirades by Jesus

against his Jewish contemporaries. Some of these are, it is true, already present in Luke's sources; but at the very least, Luke has evidently decided to include them in his Gospel and shows little inclination to modify them significantly. Thus the Q tirade against 'this generation' culminates in the doom oracle of Lk. 11.49-51, concluding the series of woes against the scribes/lawyers and Pharisees; here 'this generation' is accused of sharing (in some way) in the murderous activity of their predecessors by killing the prophets and other sent to them, 'so that this generation may be charged with the blood of all the prophets shed from the foundation of the world' (v. 50).

So too Jesus' contemporaries who have eaten and drunk with him and in whose streets he has taught (Lk. 13.26) are rejected harshly by Jesus: 'I never knew you: Depart from me all you workers of iniquity' (13.27); and the sequel in vv. 28-30, which speaks of many coming from the east and the west, the north and the south, and replacing the addressees, seems quite clearly to have in mind the latter as Jews being replaced by Gentiles. Similarly, we have seen that the parable of the Great Supper in Lk. 14.16-24 in Luke's version becomes a clear statement of Gentiles replacing Jews as the guests in the banquet (whatever may have been the meaning of the original parable).

The destruction of Jerusalem is predicted by Luke's Jesus in vivid terms in Lk. 19.34-35 (a passage peculiar to Luke), though whether this, set in the context of Jesus' weeping over the city (v. 41), is intended as implying sorrowful regret or righteous anger, is not so clear.

Perhaps more to the point is the way in which Luke seems to present at least some details of the account of Jesus' trial as if it is the Jews who are responsible for Jesus' death, perhaps even that it is the Jews who are directly instrumental in executing Jesus. In general terms it is notable that, in the passion narrative, the opposition to Jesus seems no longer to come from the Jewish leaders with the crowds being generally sympathetic (as is mostly the case earlier in the Gospel): rather, the crowds too are now hostile (cf. Lk. 23.13-25). Pilate, on the other hand, is almost friendly, and certainly portrayed as desperately anxious to release Jesus, three times declaring him innocent (Lk. 23.4, 14, 22). And in the end Pilate hands Jesus over to 'their' (= the Jews') will (v. 25), so that the decision to crucify is apparently a Jewish, not a Roman, one. Moreover, the sequel (in Lk. 23.26-33), uses general third person plurals ('*they* led him away...when *they* came...there they crucified him') which, if one interprets the syntax strictly, refer to the 'they' of v. 25, that is, the Jews.

Yet it is perhaps the story as told in Acts which contributes most to this picture of hostility to Judaism by Luke. We shall not go into many details here, but the general outline is often stereotyped and, for many, crystal clear. Stephen's speech in Acts 7 accuses the Jews of continual disobedience to God, resulting in a constant pattern of rejection and violence inflicted on God's messengers, including (by implication) Stephen himself. As the Christian mission goes into the wider world, a set pattern seems to be established as the story progresses. Regularly, the Christian missionaries start by preaching to the Jews; equally regularly the Jews reject the Christian message and stir up trouble against the Christians. As a result, the Christians are as often as not in trouble with the civic authorities, and are driven out of one city; they go to the next where the same pattern is repeated. Three times, in what appear to many as programmatic statements, Paul responds to the situation almost in exasperation, by saying that if the Jews will not listen, then the Christian mission will go to the Gentiles. This happens in Pisidian Antioch (Acts 13.46), in Corinth (Acts 18.6) and finally in the dramatic final scene in Rome, where Luke seems to save up the full quotation of Isa. 6.9-10 from Mk 4.11-12 to illustrate the apparently divinely intended Jewish refusal to respond and the apparently equally final decision now to desert the Jewish people for good: 'Let it be known to you that this salvation of God has been sent to the Gentiles: *they* will hear' (Acts 28.28).

Yet this is by no means the whole story in Luke–Acts, for balancing this apparently highly negative picture of Judaism are some equally powerful positive elements.

Pro-Judaism?

Luke is clearly steeped in Jewish Scriptures. We have already noted the way in which the theme of prophecy and

fulfilment dominates the Lukan narrative. The events of
Luke's story are thus the fulfilment of *Jewish* Scripture.
Jewish Scripture is thus part of the Christian heritage and to
be regarded thoroughly positively.

Luke's Gospel starts with the portrayal in the birth narratives of a series of figures who are presented as models of
Jewish piety, with no hint of any critique of such piety.
Further, their actions closely involve the person of Jesus.
Zachariah, the father of John the Baptist, is a priest serving
in the temple. Simeon and Anna are also based in the
temple. Jesus' parents circumcise him on the eighth day and
bring the baby to Jerusalem to offer what is apparently the
appropriate sacrifice (Lk. 2.23). So too, in the various
'prophetic' speeches/hymns (i.e. the canticles of later
Christian tradition) which are put on the lips of the characters in these birth narratives, the hope is expressed that the
arrival of John and Jesus will be the fulfilment of so many
long-standing hopes for Israel (cf. Lk. 1.54-55; 1.68-69; 2.30-
32).

The centrality of Jerusalem, and the Jerusalem temple,
continue to dominate other parts of the story. Jesus' journey
to Jerusalem is given central importance in Luke's structure
of his Gospel by his development of the travel narrative,
structured around the journey motif to which Luke gives
solemn significance at the start (9.51), with its goal as
Jerusalem, the place where a prophet 'must' meet his final
destiny (13.33). When Jesus arrives in Jerusalem, he is again
found in the temple, just as he was in the temple in the one
story Luke records of Jesus' childhood (see 2.41-51 and the
story of the 12-year-old Jesus in the temple). Thus after the
story of the 'cleansing' of the temple (which Luke drastically
abbreviates from Mark: cf. 19.45-46 par. Mk11.15-17), Luke
says that Jesus was 'teaching *daily* in the temple' (19.47):
presence in the temple is a regular pattern for the Lukan
Jesus in Jerusalem.

So too Luke rewrites parts of his tradition to ensure that
the risen Jesus appears in Jerusalem. Luke says nothing of
an appearance of Jesus in Galilee (possibly implicit in Mk
16.7, certainly explicit in Mt. 28.16-20); and he carefully
rewrites any hint of this (cf. Lk. 24.6-7, where a prophecy of a

Luke

future event in Galilee [Mk 16.7] becomes a statement about Jesus' past teachings in Galilee). Thus for Luke, the resurrection appearances are all located and focused in Jerusalem, the centre of the Jewish faith. It is then thoroughly characteristic of Luke that his final word in the Gospel has the disciples in the temple in Jerusalem continually, praising God (Lk. 24.53). The focus is entirely on the Jewish matrix of faith, with no hint of any critique.

This picture continues on in Acts (though, as before, we shall be briefer here). The early Christian community in Acts continues to worship in the temple, and carries on doing so for as long as it is allowed. Further, any critique of Jewish responsibility for inflicting violence and death on (at least some of) the Christian figures, including Jesus, is ameliorated in part by the concession that the Jews acted in ignorance (Acts 3.17; 13.27. Cf. too the prayer of Jesus on the cross in Lk. 23.34 for his executioners, who are excused because of their ignorance: 'Father, forgive them, for they do not know what they are doing'. The verse is textually uncertain, but the close parallel in the prayer of the dying Stephen in Acts 7.60 makes it likely, in view of the number of close parallels between the accounts of the deaths of Jesus and Stephen, that Lk. 23.34 is indeed a genuine part of the text of Luke's Gospel.) So too, Luke's general picture in Acts seems to be that it was only the Jewish leaders in Jerusalem who were responsible for the death of Jesus, not the Jewish people as a whole (see Matera 1990; Weatherly 1994).

Above all the positive picture of Judaism emerges from Luke's portrait of Paul in Acts. Throughout his account of Paul's career, Luke presents Paul as a law-abiding Jew, always anxious to keep the feasts in Jerusalem, concerned to have the backing of the Jewish Christian church in Jerusalem for all his endeavours, and adhering throughout to Torah observance, performing, if necessary, acts of supererogation to convince others of his attitude in this respect (cf. his paying the expenses of those who had a vow in Acts 21.23-26). In the account of the various trials and hearings which Paul undergoes in the last quarter of Acts, it is a constant motif that Paul is a law-abiding Pharisee (Acts 23.6), and that he has done nothing wrong by breaking either

Jewish or civil law (Acts 25.8). Paul is presented as *agreeing* with one major strand of Judaism, namely Pharisaism, in the one point that is portrayed as the reason for his being arrested and tried, that is, in his affirmation of a belief in resurrection which is a hope that God has given to the Jewish people as a whole. 'I stand here to be judged for the hope of the promise made by God to our fathers [i.e. resurrection]' (Acts 26.6).

Finally we may note the occasions in Acts when Luke records considerable *success* in the Christian mission among Jews. After Peter's initial sermon at Pentecost, 'about three thousand' Jews join the Christian ranks (Acts 2.41), 'about five thousand' join a little later (Acts 4.4), 'great numbers of both men and women' converts are mentioned in Acts 5.14 etc., so that when Paul arrives back in Jerusalem after his travels, James tells him 'how many thousands of believers there are among the Jews' (Acts 21.20). Even in the final scene in Acts 28, there is a mixed picture: although some Jews reject Paul's message, 'some believed' (Acts 28.24).

How then should one resolve these apparently contradictory elements in Luke's writings? Is Luke incorrigibly opposed to the Jews to the extent of being virtually 'anti-Semitic'? Or is Luke thoroughly positive about the Jews and Judaism?

Possible Solutions

The theory that Luke is thoroughly opposed to Jews, if not Judaism, has certainly had many defenders in the past, from Overbeck to scholars such as Haenchen in his monumental and highly influential commentary on Acts, and in the work of J.T. Sanders today (Sanders 1987). Thus Sanders is not afraid to accuse Luke effectively of anti-Semitism. Any positive elements in Luke's writings are simply designed as part of the narrative development leading up to the final scene in Acts 28, which expresses the final and definitive rejection of the Jewish people. The Jewish people have been found guilty of the death of Jesus, and have not taken the opportunity to repent at the offer of forgiveness in the Gospel. In Haenchen's words, 'Luke has written the Jews off' (Haenchen 1966: 278).

A rather different overall view has been presented vigorously in recent years by J. Jervell in a number of essays and articles. Jervell argues that the view of Haenchen and others does not do justice to the note of *success* among at least some Jews of the Christian mission (cf. above). The people of God is now for Luke a divided people, some having accepted the Christian message, some having rejected it. The Gentile mission is then the result of (part of) Israel having been saved. There is thus no rejection of the Jewish people in principle: rather, only those who have refused to repent are rejected. Thus the people of Israel are regarded in principle positively, and Gentiles join this repentant Israel.

Jervell is surely right to draw attention to notes of success by Christians among Jews. Yet his overall theory has a number of weaknesses. It is certainly hard to interpret verses such as Acts 13.46; 18.6 as implying that the Gentile mission results from a successful mission among Jews. The very opposite seems to be the case. So too it is not so clear that in the end, Jervell's interpretation is very different from that of the older view. Jervell too acknowledges that the scene of Acts 28 implies that the days of an appeal to Jews by Christians are for Luke past and gone: the unrepentant Jews are indeed written off as far as Luke is concerned. Thus while Jervell's Luke may have a slightly different theoretical/theological slant to Haenchen's or Sanders's Luke, as far as contemporary non-Christians Jews are concerned, there is not much difference: non-Christian Jews are no longer envisaged as likely to come into the church, and are rejected finally.

A very different interpretation has been offered by R. Tannehill, in a highly sensitive literary reading of Luke's two-volume work. Tannehill refers to the way in which the birth narratives set up hopes and expectations for the reader for things to come, much of which fails to materialize in the story Luke actually recounts. Many of these hopes and expectations are associated with those of the Jewish people for their own destiny. The angel Gabriel tells Mary that the child to be born will be given (by God!) 'the throne of David his father, and he will reign over the house of Jacob for ever' (Lk. 1.32-33). Zachariah tells of the 'redemption' of God's people and 'a horn of salvation for us in the house of his servant David' (1.68-69), and this salvation is specified later as 'salvation from our enemies' (1.71, cf. v. 74 too). Anna too speaks of the 'redemption of Jerusalem'. Moreover all these are clearly 'reliable characters' in the story of Luke–Acts. The way they are presented suggests that the reader should seriously—and positively—what they say and predict.

Yet as it develops the story indicates that these hopes fail to materialise: indeed not only in the story but in the parts of later history (future for the story, past for Luke) which are hinted at, above all the fall of Jerusalem. Luke's readers surely know that Anna's hopes of the redemption of Jerusalem have *not* materialized. Above all the Jewish people have rejected the salvation offered to them. Tannehill thus suggests that the work is presented by Luke as a tragic story, a story filled with pathos as it tells of hopes that are *not* fulfilled. And yet, as the hopes are of *God's* promises, the implication must be that the story is still open as far as the Jews are concerned, even by the end of Luke's actual story line in Acts 28. The fact that these promises are still 'on the table', still waiting to be fulfilled, and that in Luke's day there is still no sign of their being fulfilled, is what gives the story its tragic quality.

Tannehill produces many fine insights in his study; and his work shows the importance and the value of taking seriously the whole of Luke's two-volume work as a literary unity. Nevertheless it is not entirely persuasive. Whatever the element of tragedy in Luke's work, it seems that Luke in no way intends to evoke the readers' sympathy for non-Christian Jews. On a reasonably straightforward reading of Luke–Acts (if such is possible!), the sympathies of the reader seem to be drawn quite self-consciously by Luke to Jesus or the Christians who suffer at the hands of (at least some of) the Jews. Any sympathy for Jews has to be read out of quite a complex reading of Luke's work. Further, it is clear that Luke does go in for a quiet, but nevertheless quite radical, redefinition of many of the hopes expressed in the birth narratives. This comes out perhaps most clearly in some of the speeches in Acts (cf., for example, Acts 13). Here it is clear that the hopes for a new king who will produce salvation for his people *have* been fulfilled in the person of Jesus who *is* the new heir to the Davidic promises (by virtue of his resurrection) and who has brought salvation through the offer of repentance and the forgiveness of sins (see Räisänen 1991). One may wish to accuse Luke of some sleight of hand here: such fulfilment has redefined the national and political Jewish expectations in a radically individualistic way; and it could be regarded as somewhat tongue-in-cheek to say that an offer of forgiveness of sins is a radical fulfilment of Jewish eschatological expectations! (After all, is not forgiveness available anyway in Judaism?!) Nevertheless, it does seem to be the case that, for Luke, these hopes of pious people at the start of the story *are* fulfilled (at least in his eyes) in the story he does recount. For Luke there is not much idea that these hopes are still waiting to be fulfilled.

It seems hard to avoid the impression that, at least for many Jews if not for Judaism, the scene in Acts 28 is drawing a fairly firm line. Luke does not seem to hold out much more hope of any success for any Jewish mission after this time.

Is then Luke to be regarded as anti-Semitic?

In trying to answer such a question, much depends on where Luke himself is to be sited in relation to Judaism: is Luke himself an insider or an outsider? (See Salmon 1988.) For if Luke is writing from outside the fold of Judaism completely, then the negative parts of his picture of the Jews comes close to being an attack on, and rejection of, Judaism as such, so that the charge of anti-Semitism is not completely absurd. (Though one must also remember that any negative portrait of the Jews in Luke–Acts gives no encouragement at all to any policy of direct physical persecution of Jews by Christians.)

If, however, Luke is writing as an insider, from inside the fold of Judaism, then the negative elements in his story are on a par with prophetic indictments of Israel's people which have been a constant feature of Israel's history since the time of the classical prophets. Accusations of sin, apostasy, or whatever issued by Jews against other Jews by no means imply that the accusers are anti-Semitic. An Amos or an Isaiah is not anti-Semitic simply by virtue of the harsh invective used!

Yet putting the authorship question in such a way probably makes things too clear cut and black-and-white. It seems unlikely that Luke is a total outsider in relation to Judaism. The positive picture of Judaism, and the Jewish roots of the Christian story, seem to show that the author is one who is deeply in sympathy with the Jewish heritage of Christianity. Similarly, the portrait of Paul in Acts shows Luke anxious to defend his hero against any charge that he has deserted ('true') Judaism. On the other hand, it seems unlikely that Luke is a complete insider in relation to Judaism. There is a well-known catalogue of instances in the Lukan writings where Luke seems to show more than a little ignorance about some features of Jewish life. For example, Luke seems to be unclear, or inaccurate, about the legal requirements apparently being fulfilled by Mary and Joseph in 'presenting' Jesus in the temple (Lk. 2.22-24); he seems to assume that there were two high priests when Jesus' ministry begins (Lk. 3.2); and his accounts of Paul's cutting his hair because of a vow in Cenchreae (Acts 18.18), or of Paul paying the expenses of four men in Jerusalem who had a vow (Acts 21.24-26), raise well-known problems of historicity because of their lack of correspondence with what we know of Jewish practice (see the commentaries).

Perhaps the category which might fit all the evidence best is that of a 'godfearer', that is, a Gentile who is attracted by, and closely attached to Judaism by participating in synagogue worship, though without undertaking the full commitment of circumcision. (There is some debate about whether such people existed in a formal category. However, it seems likely that such people existed in general terms, even if the formal 'title', or description, of 'godfearer' is harder to establish.)

But on any showing it is clearly of vital importance for Luke to show that Christianity is in a line of almost unbroken continuity with Judaism. This is shown in the Gospel above all by the birth narratives, as we have seen; the motif of prophecy and fulfilment, emphasized above all in the programmatic scene in Nazareth (Lk. 4.21), supports it; and the picture is reinforced at the end of the Gospel by the emphasis given in the teaching of the risen Jesus to the effect that everything that has happened has been ordained by God and fulfils Scripture. So too the story in Acts as told by Luke continues in the same vein, above all in the portrait of Paul which emerges, as we have seen.

There is thus a real sense in which, for Luke, the Christian church *is* the true Israel. The pattern of prophecy and fulfilment shows the true roots of the Christian church. The opposition to the Christian movement shown by other Jews is portrayed as part of a continuous and continuing pattern of disobedience by some Jews to God's will, which has characterized Jewish history from the very start. (This is very much the burden of Stephen's speech in Acts 7: the long survey of Israelite history is to show that [some] Jews have always disobeyed and rebelled against God's messengers.) As far as 'Judaism' is concerned, therefore, there is certainly no suggestion at all that Christianity is in antithesis to Judaism. Quite the contrary!

Indeed it is not that clear that Christianity is so very new in relation to Judaism. Certainly Christianity fulfils Jewish hopes and prophecies. But there is equally as great a stress on the *continuity* between the Christian church and Israel, as Stephen's speech makes clear. It would thus not be entirely un-Lukan if the reference to the *new* covenant established by Jesus' death (Lk. 22.20) were *not* part of the Lukan text. (As we saw earlier, the verse is one of the notorious 'Western non-interpolations' in Luke's Gospel and textually uncertain; see p. 20 above.) Whatever the merits of the manuscript evidence here, the fact remains that the overall picture presented by Luke is of the one covenant, made by God with the Jewish people at Sinai; and if the Jews have disobeyed, then the Christians are the true heirs of this heritage. Luke's Paul reiterates, almost ad nauseam, that it is *Israel's* hope which is the cause of his trial, and that hope is one that is *shared* by Christians and ('true') Jews (i.e. Pharisees) alike. Given this, it is hard to accuse Luke of anti-Semitism.

Luke's Purpose

Nevertheless, there is still the further question of *why* Luke presents his story in this way. Certainly it is hard to deny that Luke has something of an axe to grind here. His picture of Paul, which is notoriously so *un*like the Paul of the letters, seems to be skewed, and perhaps deliberately so. Several answers to this problem have been suggested, though all involve an element of circularity in the argument.

Political Apologetic?

One answer given by some in the past is that the picture of the relationship between Christianity and Judaism is part of an apologetic ploy on Luke's part in relation to the Roman authorities, or to non-Jewish society in general. Thus some have argued that the picture Luke paints of almost unbroken continuity between Christianity and Judaism is aimed at a Hellenistic audience to convince them that Christianity is really true Judaism. The aim of this may then be to give the Christian religion more respectability, and perhaps legitimacy, in the eyes of a sceptical non-Jewish audience. Two slightly different underlying reasons have been suggested.

First, it may be that Christianity is claiming the same status as Judaism, as a *religio licita*: Judaism was an accepted religion and Jews were given a number of rights to be able to practise their religion. Christianity, if shown to be nothing other than true Judaism, could therefore claim the same status.

Secondly, it may be that the picture here meets a problem faced by Christians, namely, how to explain the novelty of their faith. Religions in the ancient world were many and varied, and mostly tolerated; but what was suspect was anything new. Luke's picture, by presenting Christianity as essentially Judaism, makes the implicit claim that Christianity is not new at all: it has all the antiquity of Judaism and should therefore be accorded equal respect.

Further, the picture Luke paints of consistent Jewish opposition to the Christians has the effect of showing the Roman authorities in a good light. The civic authorities are generally shown to be tolerant, or at worst indifferent, to the

Christian movement. Thus the story Luke tells may have been intended to mount a powerful piece of apologetic on behalf of the Christian church to make it acceptable to Roman, or Hellenistic, society (cf. Conzelmann 1960: 137-44).

This overall explanation may have some truth in it, though some details are unpersuasive. In particular, the notion of a *religio licita* is rather improbable, since it has been shown that such a formal category probably did not exist in the ancient world (see Maddox 1982: 91-93.). The theory that Luke is presenting a piece of political apologetic in more general terms may have an element of truth in it. Certainly the portrait of some of the civic authorities in Acts is often painted in more positive terms than is at times probable; and in the Gospel, as we have seen, Pilate is almost exonerated from any involvement in the execution of Jesus by declaring him innocent three times (see pp. 55-56 above).

On the other hand, such a theory is hard pushed to explain the whole of Luke–Acts. There is so much in the two-volume work that does not seem to be addressed to a non-Christian, Roman audience. So much of the Gospel is taken up with teaching by Jesus which is clearly addressed explicitly to the Christians of Luke's own day. Teaching on prayer (Lk. 11.2-13), on ethics (Lk. 6.20-49) or on eschatology (cf. Chapter 2 above) etc. is really not related to the theme of political apologetic. Hence the relevance and appropriateness of an often-quoted remark of C.K. Barrett: 'No Roman official would ever have filtered out so much of what to him would be theological and ecclesiastical rubbish to reach so tiny a grain of relevant apology' (1961: 63). We do not know for certain who Theophilus, the person directly addressed in Luke's two-volume work, was. But it seems much more likely that Luke is primarily addressing his work to a Christian audience.

Legitimation

With this in mind, a number of scholars have suggested that Luke is primarily addressing problems faced by Christians in his own situation via his picture of Judaism. Again the nature of the solution proposed depends critically on the alleged problem, or situation, being addressed. Thus some have argued that Luke's story serves to provide some kind of legitimation for the Christian community in a context of external threats. In the face perhaps of criticisms by non-Christian Jews creating a hostile environment, Luke's story serves to give assurance to the Christian church of its legitimacy (cf. Maddox 1982).

In a recent study, Esler (1987) has adduced a more sociological approach to argue a broadly similar case. Analogies in other situations suggest that splinter groups within larger organizations can have a variety of relationships with their parent bodies. However, at some stage the relationship can become so strained that the splinter group is almost forced to separate socially so that it becomes, in sociological terms, a sect. In response to this, and facing a situation of powerful hostility from the parent body, members of the sect may feel intense worry about the validity and self-identity of the new movement. It is precisely such a situation that Esler postulates for Luke's community: he argues that the references to powerful Jewish hostility to Jesus and the new Christian movement (cf. Lk. 4.28-30; 6.22; also the evidence of Acts) indicates that the Christians of Luke's day were facing direct antagonism from their Jewish contemporaries. Most too had originally been closely attached to Judaism, whether directly as Jews or indirectly as 'godfearers' (or the like). In this situation creating uncertainty and worry, the members of the new community needed reassurance that their decision to leave the old fold and join the new was correct. Luke's story thus provides just such legitimation for the Christian community, creating a symbolic universe, a total world view, to explain and defend the origins of the movement and its separation from its parent body (1987: esp. 46-70). So too the presentation of Christianity as an ancestral religion may have a powerful legitimating function for Gentile Christians of Luke's day (1987: 201-19).

Esler's study certainly shows the fruitfulness of adopting a less overtly theological approach and using the insights afforded by sociological analyses to throw light on a text such as Luke–Acts. However, in any such overall interpretation, seeking to explain the text in relation to its setting and vice versa, much depends on the situation of Luke's community that is proposed. Esler's model would fit very well *if* we knew for certain that the Christian community and the Jewish community had separated finally, and that the former were experiencing hostility and threat from the latter (though his persuasive arguments about the legitimating function of Luke's implied stress on the ancestral nature of Christianity does not depend on such a reconstruction in quite the same way, and hence can stand independently).

I argued above that the first of these assumptions is likely (though by no means unanimously agreed by Lukan scholars today!). I interpreted the scene in Acts 28 as implying that the era of any success among a Jewish mission seems here to be signalled as a matter of past history by Luke. Yet what of the second assumption? Is the threat faced by Luke from Jewish opponents? Such a theory is possible, and many have argued for such a situation precisely on the basis of the constant motif of *Jewish* opposition in Luke's story-world. The difficulty is to know whether Luke's story world and Luke's real world match each other so precisely.

The one point at which virtually all scholars agree that Luke allows his real world to be glimpsed is the prediction by Luke's Paul in his farewell speech to the Ephesian elders in Acts 20. Here Paul looks ahead to his future, but almost certainly to what is for Luke present reality. Paul predicts that 'savage wolves' will come in and harry the flock (v. 29) and that 'men will arise out of your midst who speak perversely in order to lead disciples astray after them' (v. 30). The trouble is that the language is rather elliptical and not at all clear. It is not certain for example whether the savage wolves are Christians or non-Christians, though the language is often used of 'heretics', rather than complete outsiders, and hence it may be that Christians, or at least people claiming to be Christians, are in view (cf. Mt. 7.15). Certainly the reference in v. 30 seems to be to Christians (cf. 'men will rise *out of your midst*').

Are these then Jewish-Christian heretics? Or are they so-called Gnostics? (We know that later, in the middle to late second century, the church was deeply divided by the presence of Gnostics.) Certainty is simply not possible, but the language here does seem to read more easily if the threat is being conceived of as involving a quite different set of ideas/people than has been the case in the story hitherto. This might then tell against the theory that Luke is trying to defend Christianity (or perhaps just his hero Paul) against hostile attacks from non-Christian Jews.

Some have argued that Luke is facing threats from Gnostics, and, for example, Paul's insistence in his farewell speech in Acts on his openness and frankness in all his preaching (Acts 20.20-21) is a quiet dig at Gnostics who are claiming secret, esoteric teaching, allegedly from Paul, as their own. Similarly, the motif of Jesus' full bodily resurrection in Luke 24 (cf. especially 24.39 and the command of Jesus to handle him and to see that he is not a ghost; also 24.43 showing Jesus physically eating) may reflect some critique of possible Gnostic claims of some kind of a spiritual, non-physical resurrection of Jesus (see Talbert 1966).

Again this seems to focus on a small part of Luke–Acts at the expense of an enormous amount elsewhere. As in the case of the theory of political apologetic on the part of Luke, such a stress on openness etc. scarcely affects large sections of Luke's work.

Anti-'Marcionite' Tendencies?

Recently, in a short article, Houlden (1984) has argued that much of the evidence of Luke's story might fit together if Luke were writing in a situation of what he regarded as dangerous tendencies among some Christians to cut themselves off from their Jewish roots entirely. We know of at least one Christian who did precisely this, namely Marcion. Marcion is almost certainly later than Luke, but it may well have been that Marcionite tendencies were present in the church at an earlier period.

In such a setting, Luke's account might make a lot of sense. If Luke's community were predominantly Gentile, and were seeking to cut their links with Judaism entirely, Luke's narrative would provide a powerful corrective. Christianity is shown to be inextricably tied to Judaism. Luke's own situation may be one in which Jewish presence is no longer a reality in his community; but the narrative then shows that the Gentile mission is a result solely of Jewish refusal to accept the gospel. It is not a result of any definitive rejection of the Jews by the Christians.

If this reconstruction is correct, then it may draw on many previous, and different, analyses of Luke–Acts. Luke may indeed be indicating in Acts the de facto break between the Christian and Jewish communities of his own day. But this is *not* in the sense of any anti-Semitism. Luke does not want to jettison the Jewish roots of the Christian faith, nor does he necessarily want to damn all contemporary Jews to oblivion, or to eternal punishment. If there is a split between the communities, it is because the Jews have rejected the gospel, not vice versa. But Luke's aim may be more pastoral, in the sense of being directed to his own community, rather than theologizing about the fate of those outside his community. Luke above all wants to show that Christians do come from a Jewish stock. Thus to quote one conclusion of one scholar (who nevertheless offers a rather different overall interpretation of Luke–Acts in other respects to the one suggested here): 'Rather than setting gentile Christianity free, Luke ties it to Judaism' (Brawley 1988: 159). Certainly this effort to tie the Christian story to its Jewish roots pervades a large part of Luke's two-volume work, as we have seen. As such, Houlden's theory may then perhaps explain more adequately than some why Luke presents the whole story in the way he has.

Further Reading

R.L. Brawley, *Luke–Acts and the Jews: Conflict, Apology, and Conciliation* (SBLMS, 33; Atlanta: Scholars Press, 1987).

P.F. Esler, *Community and Gospel in Luke–Acts* (SNTSMS, 57; Cambridge: Cambridge University Press, 1987).

L. Gaston, 'Anti-Judaism and the Passion Narrative in Luke and Acts', in P. Richardson and D. Granskou (eds.), *Anti-Judaism in Early Christianity* (Waterloo, Ontario: Wilfrid Laurier University Press, 1986), pp. 127-53.

E. Haenchen, 'The Book of Acts as Source Material for the History of Early Christianity', in Keck and Martyn (eds.), *Studies in Luke–Acts*, pp. 258-78.

J.L. Houlden, 'The Purpose of Luke', *JSNT* 21 (1984), pp. 53-65.

J. Jervell, *Luke and the Divided People of God. A New Look at Luke–Acts* (Minneapolis: Augsburg, 1972), esp. ch. 2 'The Divided People of God', pp. 41-74.

R. Maddox, *The Purpose of Luke–Acts* (Edinburgh: T. & T. Clark, 1982).

F. Matera, 'Responsibility for the Death of Jesus according to the Acts of the Apostles', *JSNT* 39 (1990), pp. 77-93.

H. Räisänen, 'The Redemption of Israel. A Salvation-Historical Perspective in Luke–Acts', in P. Luomanen (ed.), *Luke–Acts: Scandinavian Perspectives* (Helsinki: Finnish Exegetical Society, 1991), pp. 94-114.

J.T. Sanders, *The Jews in Luke–Acts* (London: SCM Press, 1987).

M. Salmon, 'Insider or Outsider? Luke's Relationship with Judaism', in Tyson (ed.), *Images of Judaism in Luke–Acts*, pp. 76-82.

C.H. Talbert, *Luke and the Gnostics* (New York: Abingdon, 1966).

R.C. Tannehill, 'Israel in Luke–Acts: A Tragic Story', *JBL* 104 (1984), pp. 69-85.

J.B. Tyson, *Images of Judaism in Luke–Acts* (Columbia: University of South Carolina Press, 1992).

—(ed.), *Luke–Acts and the Jewish People. Eight Critical Perspectives* (Minneapolis: Augsburg, 1988). (All the essays here are relevant to this chapter and provide a good representation of the varity of scholarly opinions on the issue.)

J.A. Weatherly, *Jewish Responsibility for the Death of Jesus in Luke–Acts* (JSNTSup, 106; Sheffield: JSOT Press, 1994).

S.G. Wilson, *The Gentiles and the Gentile Mission in Luke–Acts* (SNTSMS, 23; Cambridge: Cambridge University Press, 1973).

4

THE PERSON AND
WORK OF JESUS

IN THINKING AND WRITING about Luke, Luke's view on this, his theology of that, or whatever, we must not lose sight of the fact that our access to any such view or theology is at best indirect and derivative. Luke does not explicitly set out to tell us what *his* views or theology as such are. Rather, the medium he chooses is that of a story. He chooses to tell the story in Acts of aspects of the life and history of the early church; and in his Gospel he gives us a record of the life and ministry of Jesus. In discussing his Gospel, therefore, we must remember that the prime focus of attention is the person of Jesus. (This is in one sense a comment which is trite to the point of being absurdly obvious, but in the light of some discussions of Luke's theology on this or that topic, needs occasionally to be spelt out explicitly.) If then our prime focus is on Luke's Gospel, one key question must be: what does Luke think about Jesus? How does he think that Jesus is important? And perhaps a related question: why is Jesus' life (and death) important? What is it that Jesus' life and/or death have achieved? In the words of later theologizing, therefore, we need to consider Luke's Christology and, perhaps related, his soteriology. Before embarking on this, however, we must consider some methodological problems.

Methodology

How do we study the Christology of a Christian writer or thinker? One traditional answer has been to consider the use of christological titles used by the writer to refer to Jesus. Does the writer prefer one or more particular titles: Son of God, messiah or whatever? An analysis of the meaning of such titles in the background thought of the time may then give us significant insight into the christological ideas of the writer.

Such an approach has come under attack in recent years (cf. Keck 1986). On the one hand, an exclusive concentration on the use of titles may miss other, less direct ways in which an author may wish to signal the significance of Jesus. On the other hand, a titular approach is in danger of assuming that titles applied to Jesus are, if not univocal, at least unchanging in their potential meanings; if one is not careful, one may assume that a title carries with it a constant and unchanging range of meaning whereby, when the title is applied to Jesus, it is assumed that this meaning is being ascribed to him.

Such an approach is, of course, misleading. Some titles are, of course, multivalent (though that in itself would not matter: it would just be a question of sorting out which, among a discrete and limited range of options, the relevant meaning was in each case). More importantly, it is almost certainly the case that many titles, or descriptions, when applied by Christians to Jesus, significantly changed their meaning. Hence sometimes it would seem that Jesus' own life and person determine the meaning of the Christian use of a significant term quite as much as any usage in the background.

All these problems are particularly relevant in the case of the Lukan writings. A vital part of the significance of Jesus for Luke is the fact that Jesus has been raised from the dead. And although, as we shall see, this is integrally related in Luke's writings to a number of christological titles, it is not exhausted by any one title and indeed is in part determinative of the meaning of some of the titles.

So too it is not always clear how much Luke is aware of the background meaning of some of the titles used of Jesus. In at least one case, it seems that it is the story of Jesus which determines what is said of the titles, quite as much as the reverse (cf. below on the link between messiahship and suffering). So too Luke may at times run some of the titles together. All of them are, of course, predicated of Jesus, but it is not always clear that Luke has necessarily compartmentalized the meaning and significance of the various terms and categories used by characters in his story with the same precision as all his modern interpreters.

Above all we must remember that Luke is not writing a doctrinal treatise on Christology, nor does he write a book, or a doctoral thesis, on his theology with a neat summary chapter on Christology. What he does write is a story, a narrative, and anything he wishes to say has to be communicated via that medium. This means that, as often as not, Luke's views emerge only indirectly, by more subtle hints and allusions, and by narrative structures and plot development, rather than by a neatly structured model student essay with clear subheadings and numbered, bulleted points.

Yet despite all these caveats, we must also remember that Luke's chosen medium of narrative, even if not a doctrinal treatise, still uses words, and it conveys its meaning verbally. Moreover, it is clear that very often the significance of Jesus is articulated in Luke's story by means of the use of key titles applied to Jesus. Thus, while being fully aware of the difficulties and dangers inherent in a titular approach to the Christology of a writer such as Luke, we cannot ignore titles completely. Not only does Luke use them, but they also can serve as a very useful way of categorizing our own ideas, and providing us with a reference grid, to enable us to distinguish different ideas and concepts. Thus, as a way of getting into the subject, I shall adopt a titular approach here, simply as a useful reference point, though one must be fully alive to the limitations of such an approach and also be wary of assuming that any one title has a fixed meaning.

Luke's writings also present considerable further difficulties in this context for other reasons as well. In one way Luke is similar to the other evangelists in that they all communicate their message via the medium of an account of the life of Jesus. It is something of a commonplace now to say that the evangelists are theologians of some sort, and have influenced the story they tell to get their own particular message across. The question though is: how much has this happened? How far has Luke allowed his own ideas to colour his presentation? Conversely, how far can we take the presentation in Luke's own story as a full treatment of Luke's own Christology?

Such questions arise in the case of all the four evangelists. But with Luke there is the added complication due to the existence of Acts. I have said repeatedly that Acts cannot be ignored in assessing Luke's ideas and concerns. Now Acts is rich in material to do with Christology, both in general terms (i.e. concerning the significance of Jesus' life and death) as well as the more specific christological material contained there, especially in the speeches. Yet the Acts material presents particular problems here, since it is not always clear how much Luke's own theology is reflected and how much is due to Luke's tradition. There need be no dichotomy between the two, and we have already noted that Luke's willingness to include traditional material may be just as significant in any assessment of his concerns as any positive changes he makes (see p. 26 above). Nevertheless, the fact that the Gospel and Acts together present such a variety of views, especially over the question of Christology, should at least alert us to the possibility that we cannot simply read Luke's Christology from an amalgam of the whole material in Luke–Acts.

Again, Luke, and Luke's Gospel, cannot be interpreted in isolation from Acts, and the area of Christology is no exception. But on the question of the differences and agreements of Luke's Gospel and Acts it is striking how much Luke seems at times to be sensitive (to say the least) to the context of the story world he is narrating at any one point. Jesus' preaching in the Gospel is frequently about the kingdom of God; in Acts references to the kingdom are far less frequent. In the Gospel Jesus refers to himself as Son of Man on more than 20 occasions; in Acts, there is just one reference to Jesus as Son of Man (Acts 7.56). Conversely, the speeches in Acts are full of exhortations to repent so that people may receive the forgiveness of sins; such language is not lacking in the Gospel, but it is far less prominent. Luke thus seems to show that he is aware of the different categories used by various people in his story and he seeks not to confuse them.

Even within Acts, Luke may show some considerable sensitivity, or literary skill (whatever one decides to call it). The speeches in Acts are often regarded as Lukan compositions through and through; yet it is still the case that Luke seems to show sensitivity about what his characters can or should appropriately say. Significantly it is Paul, and only Paul, in Acts who is made to say something about justification and faith (Acts 13.42), even if what is said is in the end rather un-Pauline: still Luke seems to know something of the characteristic vocabulary of his characters and he does not confuse them.

Such a view has been developed in an important essay by Moule (1966) on the Christology of Acts. As we shall see, some details of his argument are perhaps questionable (cf. below on 'Lord'), but in general terms his thesis is persuasive: Luke writes a life-like narrative (which is *not* necessarily the same as a historically accurate narrative); thus when we read the words of a character in the story, we hear as much what Luke thinks the character would have said as what Luke himself might have said.

Luke's Christology

With these methodological caveats, we may turn to the topic of this chapter, that is, the significance of Jesus for Luke, and as already said, despite the methodological dangers outlined above, I shall approach the topic via the use of key terms, or titles, applied to Jesus in Luke's story. I start with the term 'Lord'.

Lord
One of the most frequently used titles to refer to Jesus in Luke–Acts is 'Lord' (Greek *Kyrios*). This occurs very often in both of Luke's books and may be regarded as one of his most characteristic christological terms. To be sure, it is not very distinctive within early Christianity: the term is very common in Pauline Christianity as well. Nevertheless, this cannot hide the importance for the term for Luke.

Moule (1966: 160-61) has sought to discern a significant distinction in Luke's use of the term between the Gospel and

Acts. Recognizing that *Kyrios* almost certainly represents Luke's own Christology from a post-resurrection perspective, Moule nevertheless argues that the usage in the Gospel is different. Distinguishing between a use in the vocative ('O Lord'), which in Greek need only be a polite form of address (equivalent roughly to our English 'Sir!'), and the use in other cases (e.g. 'The Lord said'), Moule points to the fact that virtually no human characters in the story refer to Jesus as Lord in an obviously christologically significant way: they only use the vocative; the nominative and other cases are used by the narrator (though Elizabeth in Lk. 1.43 may be an exception to this rule). Hence, it is argued, Luke is clearly distinguishing his own perspective from the pre-Easter situation, and Luke does not seem to be reading back his own viewpoint into the pre-Easter story.

In general terms this might be persuasive, but some instances in the Gospel suggest that the picture is more complex. On at least two occasions, a vocative usage is placed just next to a non-vocative. Thus in Lk. 19.8, Zacchaeus says 'to the Lord', 'Look half of my possessions, Lord, I will give to the poor' (cf. also Lk. 12.41, 42). The vocative usage gains considerably in significance by virtue of its juxtaposition with the non-vocative usage. The one who is addressed as Lord is precisely *the* Lord. Hence we probably cannot distinguish the Gospel from Acts quite so easily.

What though does the word signify for Luke? The Greek word *Kyrios* has an enormous breadth of possible meaning, ranging from a polite form of address, through a reference to the master of a slave, to the gods of Hellenistic cults, right up to the point where is was (almost certainly) used by Greek-speaking Jews to refer to Yahweh himself. Where within this spectrum—from very human to absolutely divine—does Luke's use of *Kyrios* to refer to Jesus lie?

The answer is probably somewhere in the middle. Luke's usage in Acts is in fact notoriously imprecise, so that it is often uncertain whether a reference to *Kyrios* is intended to refer to God or Jesus. But the very existence of such confusion suggests that, for Luke, at least some of the attributes or functions of God are now conceived as being exercised by Jesus. Thus, for example, the Spirit, which is regarded in

Acts 2.17 as a gift of God, is said to be the gift of Jesus in Lk. 24.49.

On the other hand, it would probably be quite wrong to see this as necessarily ascribing divinity as such to Jesus. Such categories would probably be quite alien to Luke. Much more significant is probably the fact of the resurrection in establishing Jesus' Lordship. The logic is spelt out in Peter's speech in Acts 2 and its reference to Ps. 110.1 ('The Lord said to my Lord, Sit at my right hand...'). According to Luke's Peter, the resurrection shows that Jesus has fulfilled this text since he is now at God's right hand—hence he is appropriately called 'Lord'; or in the words of v. 36: 'God has made him Lord...' Thus it is primarily by virtue of the resurrection, and the fulfilment of Scripture, that Jesus is shown to be Lord. Again we see the crucial significance of the fulfilment motif for Luke.

This does, however, create something of a tension with the picture in the Gospel where frequently Luke presents Jesus as Lord already, prior to the resurrection. For example, Elizabeth speaks of Mary as 'the mother of my Lord' (Lk. 1.43), the angel proclaims the birth of Jesus as that of 'Christ, the Lord' (2.11), and Luke, as we have seen, in his role as the narrator frequently refers to Jesus as Lord in his Gospel.

The use of 'the Lord' by the narrator need be no problem and is no more anachronistic than saying 'Mrs Thatcher left school at the age of 18' (when of course she was not yet married and hence was not called Mrs Thatcher). Texts like Lk. 1.43; 2.11 are, however, more difficult, and there is no easy answer to what is a standing problem for all studies of Lukan Christology. The resurrection is of crucial significance for Luke in establishing Jesus' position and status for the post-Easter church, and yet that status seems to be already attained prior to Easter. (It is, of course, not so different from many other parts of the New Testament: cf. the Philippian hymn of Phil. 2.5-11). Nor is it confined to Luke's use of *Kyrios*: it is there too in the next term we shall consider, 'messiah'.

Messiah

Again this is a very common terms in Luke–Acts: Jesus is the *Christos*, the anointed messiah of Judaism. ('Messiah' is the transliteration of the Hebrew word *mashiah*, meaning an anointed figure, the Greek equivalent being *Christos*, from where we get our English usage 'Christ'.) As with *Kyrios*, Luke shares this description of Jesus as *Christos* with a wide range of other early Christians: there is no doubt that the term was applied to Jesus at a very early date and became so firmly attached to him that, also at a very early date, it often lost virtually all of its original connotation and became just a proper name (as in 'Jesus Christ', 'Christ Jesus', or even just 'Christ', as in the very early pre-Pauline formula in 1 Cor. 15.3).

Luke's own slant on the term comes in at least two ways. First, as with *Kyrios*, the resurrection and the fulfilment of Scripture are vital keys in the ascription of the term 'Christ' to Jesus. Again the Pentecost speech of Acts 2 is crucial, this time in relation to Ps. 16.10, cited in vv. 27, 31 ('You will not abandon my soul to Hades, or let your Holy One experience corruption'). This is assumed to refer to the messiah (since it manifestly cannot apply to David himself since David died and was buried: cf. v. 29); since Jesus by his resurrection has not been allowed to 'experience corruption', he must be the messiah of the psalm. Hence the other half of the conclusion in Acts 2.36: 'God has made him both Lord *and messiah*'. Thus once again we see the importance of the fulfilment motif for Luke.

But secondly, Luke adds another significant twist to his talk of Jesus as messiah by insisting that Jesus' suffering and death are necessary functions of the messiah as foretold in Scripture. This is said by the risen Jesus to the disciples on the road to Emmaus (Lk. 24.26-27), and is repeated again by Peter and Paul in Acts (Acts 3:18; 17.3; 26.23). It is, in fact, universally agreed that there are no instances in the Old Testament of a messiah figure having to suffer, let alone die. (Figures such as the suffering servant of Isa. 53 are not messiah figures.) What has almost certainly happened is that Luke has brought together his beliefs (a) that Jesus is the messiah and (b) that Jesus fulfils Scripture with (c) the brute fact of Jesus' suffering and death to produce the somewhat artificial scheme that 'the messiah must suffer'. Thus once again we see Luke's concern for the motif of fulfilment; but we also see a good illustration of the way in which titles may well change their significance when applied to Jesus. The events of Jesus' life and death may themselves determine the meaning of the description, quite as much as vice versa.

What else Luke may have understood by the term is not certain. Messianic expectations in the first century were in a state of considerable flux, and it was by no means the case that Jews of the period had a monolithic expectation of a single figure called 'the messiah'. As we have seen, a messianic figure is simply one who is anointed, and anointing could take place in a variety of contexts. One such context was certainly that of a royal figure: a new king was anointed, and so a messianic figure could be a royal person, in Judaism then a descendant of David and a new king who would restore the political fortunes of the people.

There is a little of such expectation reflected in Luke, though not a great deal. The idea of Jesus as Son of David, which occurs elsewhere in the New Testament, surfaces only occasionally here, mostly in the birth narratives. Thus the angel Gabriel tells Mary that the son to be born will be given 'the throne of his ancestor David', and 'he will reign over the house of Jacob for ever' (Lk. 1.33-34). Zachariah proclaims that God 'has raised up a mighty saviour for us, in the house of his servant David' (1.69); and Joseph is said to be of Davidic descent (1.27; 2.4; cf. 3.23ff.). Luke also takes over from Mark the cry to Jesus by blind Bartimaeus 'Jesus, Son of David, have mercy on me' (Lk. 18.38 = Mk 10.48). But elsewhere not a lot is made of any Davidic descent of Jesus by Luke.

The royal idea is also not absent from Luke, though it is not very prominent. Royal/political hopes are clearly raised in the birth narratives (Lk. 1.33; 1.69). But it is equally clear through the rest of the story that whatever benefits and blessings Jesus brings, they are not in the form of political involvement, let alone any military or political victory, for Israel. The explicit idea of Jesus as a king rarely surfaces— though it does come once (redactionally) in Luke's account of the triumphal entry, where Luke rewrites Mark's 'Blessed is the one who comes in the name of the Lord' (Mk 11.9) to become 'Blessed is the king who comes in the name of the Lord' (Lk. 19.38). But the context in which the saying is placed—Jesus riding into Jerusalem on a donkey—makes it crystal clear that any kingship of Jesus is *not* that of a politically powerful ruler.

Similarly, in the passion narrative, Jesus is accused of being a king before Pilate (Lk. 23.2), but alongside two other charges that are (for Luke) clearly false (perverting the nation, and forbidding the payment of taxes); hence Jesus' kingship is at the very least quite unlike the kingship that would threaten Pilate's political power directly. On the cross, Jesus is mocked as King (Lk. 23.36-37 in dependence on Mark), but, as before, the context indicates that, insofar as the taunt is true, Jesus' kingship is not that of this-worldly political power. So too the suggestion that Jesus is a king and thereby a threat to the political status quo is raised in Acts 17.7, but in a context which suggests that this is a wrong assessment of the situation.

Luke thus seems to be aware of royal language being ascribed to Jesus, and in part he adopts it, but only by also playing down any political associations linked with such language.

In Judaism, priests were also anointed, but there is nothing in Luke similar to the argument of Hebrews that Jesus is a priestly figure (and in Hebrews Jesus is not explicitly presented a 'Christ' figure, i.e. an anointed person, by virtue of his [high-]priesthood).

The third class of anointed figures in Judaism is that of prophets (cf. Ps. 105.15; 2 Kgs 1.9), and it is this which in part Luke seems to have adopted positively. We turn therefore to the idea of Jesus as a prophetic figure in Luke.

Prophet
Luke is the one New Testament writer to explain in a little more detail just how he conceives of Jesus being anointed. Kings and priests are of course anointed with oil. Luke conceives of Jesus as anointed with the Spirit. This is announced by Jesus himself in the opening scene in Nazareth where he

quotes the words from Isa. 61.1-2: 'The Spirit of the Lord is
upon me, because he has anointed me...', and then asserts
they have been fulfilled in the today of his presence (Lk. 4.17,
21). This claim is echoed by Peter later in Acts 10.38: 'God
anointed Jesus of Nazareth with the Holy Spirit and with
power'. Further, the fact that these words from Isaiah 61 are
in the Old Testament the words of a prophet, and the evidence we now have from some Qumran texts about the way
in which this verse from Isaiah 61 was being used by other
Jews of this period to refer to a prophetic figure, suggests
very strongly that what is in mind here is a *prophetic*
anointing. Jesus is presented as the one anointed by the
Spirit to be a *prophet*. It is thus the prophetic, rather than
royal, overtones which therefore come to the fore in the
specific anointing experienced by Jesus, according to Luke's
telling of the story.

The category of prophet certainly comes out elsewhere in
the Gospel strongly. Later on in the scene in Nazareth, Jesus
uses the examples of Elijah and Elisha working outside the
confines of Israel to illustrate the proverb that 'no prophet is
accepted in the prophet's own *patris*' (Lk. 4.24), which is evidently regarded as applicable to his own situation. Clearly
then Jesus is seen as a prophet and, as such, finds no
welcome in his own home place.

In the story of the raising of the widow of Nain's son
(Lk. 7.10-17), a story peculiar to Luke and with many echoes
of the story of Elijah raising the widow of Zarephthah's son
(1 Kgs 17.17-24), the crowd acknowledge Jesus at the end
with the words 'A great prophet has risen among us' (v. 16).
Jesus in his ministry is thus seen by others, and almost
certainly by Luke, as a prophet, recapitulating the work of
the prophets of the past.

Similarly in the story of the sinful woman (Lk. 7.36-50)
which comes shortly afterwards, the prophetic aspect comes
out once again. The Pharisee, in whose house Jesus is, says
'If this man were a prophet, he would have known what kind
of woman that is who is touching him—that she is a sinner'
(v. 39). But the rest of the story makes it very clear that
Jesus knows perfectly well exactly what kind of a woman
this is, and hence by implication he really is a prophet.

In the middle of the long journey to Jerusalem, solemnly announced at Lk. 9.51, Jesus claims that he *must* reach his goal in the city of Jerusalem 'because it is impossible for a prophet to be killed outside of Jerusalem' (Lk. 13.33): again this a tradition which occurs in Luke alone.

Luke also takes over from Mark the notes of the speculations by Herod and the crowds about whether John or Jesus might be a prophet. It may be significant that Luke slightly alters Mark in the second case. In Mark, the disciples echo the speculations of the crowds about Jesus that he might be a prophet. By implication, the structure of the story suggests that such views are wrong, and Peter articulates the better (i.e. for the evangelist) view that Jesus is the messiah. Luke has the same structure of the pericope as Mark, but he has the disciples say that the crowds think that 'one of the ancient prophets has arisen'. Thus what is implicitly denied is not so much that Jesus is a prophet per se, but that he is one of the ancient prophets returning. The latter then leaves open the possibility that Jesus himself *is* a prophet, a term which in Luke's understanding is not then necessarily antithetical to the view that Jesus is God's messiah (Lk. 9.20) or anointed one since he is anointed with the Spirit.

Finally in the Gospel, we may note the words placed on the lips of the disciples on the road to Emmaus, who say that Jesus 'was a prophet mighty in deed and word before God and all the people' (Lk. 24.19). They also note that he has been crucified and that they had hoped that he would 'redeem Israel' (v. 21). Jesus' reply is in terms of the necessity of the messiah to suffer (v. 26). But the stress is on the necessity of the suffering: it is not on the fact that Jesus is messiah and not prophet. Thus the Christological category of prophet is not questioned by the story, even if the role and activity of the person concerned is quietly corrected.

In Acts the prophetic category for Jesus comes at two critical points, in Acts 3.22-23 and 7.37, where the prediction by Moses of 'a prophet like me' who is to come in the future (Deut. 18.15) is quoted and clearly by implication applied to Jesus. Jesus is thus presented not just as any old prophet, but specifically as the prophet like Moses, expected on the basis of the verse in Deuteronomy 18. (We now know from a

Qumran text, 4QTest, that this verse from Deuteronomy had led to expectations by some Jews of a prophet like Moses who would come in the future.)

Luke's portrayal of Jesus as a prophet in the Gospel may thus be significantly influenced by the idea of Jesus as the prophet like Moses. Such influence may also be seen in a few details of Luke's account apart from the explicit references to Jesus as prophet we have noted already. For example, in Luke's account of the transfiguration story, Luke adds to Mark the note that Moses and Elijah were speaking with Jesus 'of his departure which he was about to accomplish in Jerusalem' (Lk. 9.31). The Greek word for 'departure' here is *exodos*, with clear echoes of the Moses story: Jesus' 'journey' to Jerusalem is thus portrayed as a new 'exodus' journey, recapitulating the first 'exodus' by the first Moses. So too the command of the voice from heaven 'Listen to him!' (Lk. 9.35) is aligned by Luke more closely to the command of Deut. 18.15 itself.

The importance of the 'prophet like Moses' theme for Luke has been strongly stressed by a number of scholars in recent studies. Johnson (1977) has argued that the pattern of Moses as set out in Stephen's speech has heavily influenced Luke's presentation and provides the key pattern to the whole of the structure of Luke–Acts. Moses is sent by God, rejected by the people, and then raised up again, but rejected a second time. So too Jesus, the prophet like Moses, is sent by God, rejected by his people, but raised up by God (i.e. in the resurrection); the mission goes out a second time to the people, this time in the form of the mission of the disciples sent out by Jesus, but is again rejected. This pattern of double mission and double rejection finds its logic in the Mosaic typology.

The theory is attractive, though not fully persuasive in all its details. The parallel in the second mission becomes less close, since Jesus himself is no longer a direct participant in the mission: it is rather the disciples who go out in Jesus' name. Nevertheless the pattern of prophecy, and prophecy rejected, is clearly one which has heavily influenced Luke's presentation in his Gospel, with the Mosaic category providing an important greater precision.

A similar thesis has been propounded by Moessner (1989)

who has argued that at least the model of a single prophetic ministry and prophetic rejection can find its origin in the Mosaic pattern. Moessner has also argued that the great Central Section, or Travel Narrative, in Luke (Lk. 9.51–18.14) may be based on the book of Deuteronomy, so that Jesus is here presented on a grand scale as the prophet like Moses.

The parallels between Deuteronomy and the Central Section in Luke have been noted by others before Moessner (cf. Evans 1955), though Moessner's book is probably the most detailed and fullest working out of the theory. One wonders if at times the theory becomes almost too specific. The parallels are at times rather general, and it is not clear how far an ancient reader would have picked them up. Nevertheless, whatever one makes of the detailed structure of the Travel Narrative, the general theory seems justified that, for Luke, Jesus is a prophet, and the prophet like Moses. Like Moses (though also like many other prophets) Jesus experiences rejection. Thus Luke uses the Q traditions in Lk. 11.49-51; 13.34-35 which express the idea that all God's prophets have suffered rejection, violence and even death. Luke (and Q) is probably echoing a very widespread tradition in Judaism which had developed such an idea within a deuteronomistic view of history, referring to the violence suffered by the prophets as illustrating the continuing disobedience of the people, but using this as the basis for an appeal to repent and change their ways.

Luke's view of Jesus as a prophet is thus a very important theme for him. It surfaces explicitly on a number of occasions and may also be related, as we have seen, to a number of other details in Luke's story, as well as to the use of the messianic category. It is however by no means the only category used by Luke, and some of these other themes we shall consider briefly here.

Son of God

Perhaps one of the most perplexing problems of Luke's Christology is his use of the term Son of God to refer to Jesus. The term is not used very frequently—certainly in Acts it is far less common than *Kyrios* or *Christos*. Many of the uses in the Gospel are already present in Luke's sources. Certainly it is very hard to find any clear consistency in Luke's use of the phrase.

For example, in some instances the phrase is used in a messianic way, to refer to Jesus as messiah. Perhaps what is in mind is a royal idea of messiahship (though we have seen that a prophetic idea of messiahship in Luke is equally strong if not stronger), with the idea of the Davidic king as son of God (cf. Ps. 2.7; 2 Sam. 7.14). Thus in Lk. 4.41, Luke adds a clarification to Mark's account of Jesus' rebuking the demons who cried out that he was the Son of God 'because they knew him' (Mk 1.39) so that it is now 'because they knew that he was the messiah' (Lk. 4.41). 'Son of God' and 'messiah' seem here to be virtually equated. Similarly, the angel's words to Mary in Lk. 1.32 seem to equate divine sonship with a royal Davidic position: 'He will be called the Son of the Most High, and the Lord God will give him the throne of his ancestor David'.

On the other hand, in Luke's account of the Sanhedrin trial, what is in Mark a single question to Jesus 'Are you the messiah, the Son of the Blessed One?' (Mk 14.61) becomes in Luke two separate questions, asking what appear to be thought of as two different things: 'If you are the messiah, tell us' (Lk. 22.67), and 'Are you then the Son of God?' (Lk. 22.69). In Mark, the parallelism in the single question seems to imply that the two terms are regarded as virtually synonymous. The separation of the two into different questions in Luke seems to imply that 'messiah' and 'Son of God' are distinct titles with different connotations.

Luke also takes over from Q the temptation story with the Devil addressing Jesus as Son of God (Lk. 4.1-13), and the cry of exaltation (Lk. 10.21-22) where Jesus addresses God as Father and refers to himself as Son as the mediator of exclusive revelation.

When exactly Jesus becomes Son is not clear either. In one of the speeches in Acts, Luke has Paul cite Ps. 2.7 ('You are my son, today I have begotten you'), applied apparently to the moment of Jesus' resurrection (Acts 13.32). This would suggest that Jesus becomes Son of God at and by virtue of his resurrection. On the other hand, Luke has God's voice from heaven declare Jesus as His Son at the Jesus' baptism (Lk. 3.22—*possibly* with the words 'today I have begotten you': this is the reading of the Western text, though the Alexandrian texts read 'with you I am well pleased', as in Mark). And the angel tells Mary in the birth narratives that because of her conception by the Holy Spirit, the child to be born will be holy and 'will be called Son of God' (Lk. 1.35). Both these latter passages suggest that Jesus is already Son of God in his pre-Easter existence. We have thus the same ambiguity that we noticed when looking at the use of *kyrios* as applied to Jesus.

The background of the term 'Son of God' is enormously varied. Certainly the phrase on its own does not imply necessarily any divinity as such (although it became the vehicle for expressing Jesus' divinity in later Christian language). A son of God in Judaism could be a royal human figure (cf. Ps. 2.7; 2 Sam. 7.14), or even a faithful, obedient human being (Sir. 4.11; Wis. 2.15). Luke too knows this kind of language, since followers of Jesus can be sons of God (cf. Lk. 6.35), and they too can address God as Father (Lk. 11.2).

Some of Luke's confused picture here might be explained on source-critical grounds: many of the references to Jesus as Son of God clearly come from his sources Mark and Q; others may come from other sources he has available (e.g. his account of the Sanhedrin trial). But one cannot drive too much of a wedge between Luke and his sources: after all, he did decide to include them in his Gospel (cf. p. 26 above)! Perhaps consistency is unattainable; but clearly Luke knows of the tradition that Jesus is thought of as Son of God, and he does develop it in different ways.

Son of Man

There is no space here to discuss the vexed question of what the term Son of Man meant on the lips of Jesus, and Luke's use of the term can be dealt with only briefly (see further Tuckett 1995).

Luke knows and uses almost all his sources' (Mark's and Q's) uses of the term. He adds quite a number of his own (Lk. 17.22; 18.8; 19.10; 21.36; 22.22; 22.48; Acts 7.56), many (if not all) of which may well be his own redactional

creations. Yet, with the exception of Acts 7.56, these are all
in the Gospel: Luke perhaps knows that 'Son of Man' was not
a widely used term in the church's preaching, and he uses his
literary/ historical sensitivity by not writing the term into
the story in Acts. Similarly, all his additional (i.e. to Mark
and Q) uses of the term occur in contexts that are very
similar to those of his sources, namely to refer to the
suffering of Jesus and his vindication/exaltation, as well as
his mission to save (Lk. 19.10 cf. Mk 10.45). Luke thus has
developed and expanded the range of Son of Man sayings;
but he has not significantly altered the basic slant of his
source material.

Servant

Finally, in this list of categories, we may consider the
application in Luke–Acts to Jesus of language associated
with the suffering servant passage of Isaiah 53 (this is
scarcely a title).

It is perhaps one of the surprising features of the New
Testament that Isaiah 53 is used so rarely to interpret Jesus'
life and death. Luke does have a few references to the
servant passages. For example, in the Nunc Dimittis, Simeon
echoes the words of the third servant song in predicting that
Jesus will be 'a light to lighten the Gentiles' (Lk. 2.32 cf. Isa.
49.6), although it is not certain if Luke, or his readers, would
have associated together what modern scholarship has
identified as *the* four servant songs.

In a passage peculiar to Luke in his passion narrative,
Luke has Jesus say that the saying of Scripture 'He was
counted among the lawless' must be fulfilled in his case
(Lk. 22.37), and this Scripture is Isa. 53.12, that is, part of
the fourth servant song.

A few passages in Acts carry on the theme. Thus Peter in
Acts 3.13 claims that God 'glorified his servant', language
that is reminiscent of Isa. 52.13. (However, the references to
Jesus as 'servant' in Acts 4.27 seem to be in a context of
Jesus as a Davidic figure and may reflect the language of
David as God's servant.) In Acts 8.32-33, Isa. 53.7-8 is cited
in extenso as the words being read by the Ethiopian eunuch,
who subsequently has the passage explained to him by Philip
as being a reference to the person of Jesus.

References to Jesus as the servant are thus present in Luke–Acts, and indeed are more numerous than in the other Gospels, but are still not extensive. It is perhaps part of Luke's general fulfilment motif: Jesus fulfils the role of many Old Testament figures. But it is by no means the only, and certainly not the most dominant, example of this in Luke–Acts.

The significance of the Servant idea does, however, raise by implication a more wide-ranging question, namely, what does Luke think that the life and/or death of Jesus have achieved? The issue is raised by the possible Servant Christology, because Isaiah 53 is about the only passage in the Old Testament where the suffering of a person is said to be vicarious, benefitting others by in some sense suffering instead of them. Now it is of course a well-known feature of early Christianity, especially Pauline Christianity, that it too claimed that Jesus' death was vicarious: it was 'for us', or 'for our sins'. In itself this makes it all the more surprising in many ways that Isaiah 53 was not explicitly used more often by early Christians in their talk about Jesus' death. What then of Luke?

The Significance of Jesus' Death

Luke is notorious for having so little to say at one level about the significance of Jesus' death. All the Synoptic evangelists are somewhat reticent, to say the least, about any positive significance in Jesus' death. Luke is even more so. Mark has two sayings which seem to attribute saving significance to Jesus' death: Mk 10.45 ('the Son of Man came...to give his life a ransom for many'), and the saying over the cup at the Eucharist in Mk 14.24 ('This is my blood of the covenant, which is poured out for many'). Luke famously (or infamously) has no direct parallel to the ransom saying in Mk 10.45b: he either rewrites, or has an independent tradition of, the verse in Lk. 22.27 which focuses on the substance of only the first half of Mk 10.45 and speaks of the importance of serving; and Luke's parallel to Mk 14.24 in Lk. 22.20 is a famous Western non-interpolation: hence it is not certain if this is part of the genuine text of Luke's Gospel (see p. 20 above). There are no other texts in the Gospel which ascribe positive, saving significance to Jesus' death.

Nor is there much, if any, evidence of this in Acts. Only one verse really seems relevant: in Paul's speech to the Ephesian elders he speaks of 'the church of God which he obtained with the blood of his own Son' (Acts 20.28), which might suggest ideas of purchasing or redemption. But this is about the only verse where the topic is mentioned explicitly. The use of Isaiah 53 in Acts 8 is famous for the fact that the actual verses cited from Isaiah 53 (vv. 7-8 cited in Acts 8.32-33) are not those which actually mention the specifically vicarious nature of the servant's suffering. (It is though unclear whether they are implied: is the citation of one extract from the chapter intended to evoke the whole of the rest of the chapter in the reader's mind? The issue is a debated one, and not easily resolvable.)

Luke then would seem to imply that Jesus' death in itself is not of the same central significance as it is given by Paul (or John or Mark for that matter). Now one can argue that, just as Luke does not present us with a treatise on Christology, he does not give us an essay on soteriology either. Instead he writes a story, and, as we have seen, it is in literary or historical terms often a very sensitively written story. Luke makes his characters say what he thinks that it is appropriate for them to say in the contexts in which he places them in his story world. Thus, in relation to soteriology, it may be that teaching about the significance of Jesus' death did not characterize early Christian missionary preaching to outsiders, but was more a feature of in-house teaching to those already converted. Could it then be no coincidence that the only reference to Jesus' death in Acts is in the one speech made to those already converted, while it is missing from the other speeches which are addressed to outsiders?

This is certainly possible, and many have argued in this way, though the relative silence in the Gospel, where much of the teaching is evidently directed to those who are already Christian disciples, is still surprising. The silence has given rise to a number of claims by scholars that in Luke 'there is indeed no *theologia crucis* beyond the affirmation that the Christ must suffer, since so the prophetic Scriptures foretold'

(Creed 1930: lxxii). This is perhaps not entirely fair, and probably expects more from Luke and his chosen genre than may be appropriate. Luke is not Paul; nor is Luke's medium of story the same as Paul's medium of doctrinal letter. Nevertheless one must say that the relative silence of such ideas, in the Acts material especially, does suggest that Luke does have a rather different slant on things.

If one asks of the Lukan writings what has been achieved by Jesus' death, the answer is very often in relatively general terms. As far as vocabulary is concerned, it is clear that the language of salvation is extremely important for Luke. It is a constant feature of the speeches in Acts that people may be 'saved', or receive 'salvation', as we have already seen; and Jesus is explicitly called a 'saviour' on a few occasions. Thus the angel tells the shepherds that 'to you is born this day in the city of David a Saviour' (Lk. 2.11), a term echoed twice in Acts (Acts 5.31; 13.23). Yet precisely how this salvation is achieved, or how (if at all) it directly relates to Jesus' death, is not spelt out.

The second main benefit resulting from the Christ-event is the forgiveness of sins, again a motif which concludes many of the speeches of Acts. The fact that the Christ-event somehow deals with sin/sins and its/their effects is, of course, common to Luke, Paul and many others in early Christianity. But again one has to say that any specific theory about how such forgiveness is made available though what Jesus has done, either in his life or his death, is left open. Indeed, as already noted, it could be seen as somewhat tongue-in-cheek to suggest that Jews almost need to be converted to another religion (or a special event associated with Jesus) to receive forgiveness of their sins! (However, the extent to which Christianity is another religion for Luke is of course debatable: see Chapter 3 above.)

Perhaps though, if Luke is rather vague here, he is by no means unique. Even Paul's more explicit statements about the meaning of the death of Jesus defy logic when examined closely. They represent rather a rich variety of an almost riotous mixture of metaphors and images (Jesus' death as a sin offering, a covenant sacrifice, a ransom price paid [to whom?!], a victory over the Devil etc.). No doubt what was

primary was the experience of early Christians of the new
life they claimed was theirs, made possible, they believed, in
and through the death and resurrection of Jesus. The means
by which this happened came from later attempts at
rationalization (see Tuckett 1992). If Luke's rationalizing
goes on a different track from Paul's then that maybe simply
shows that Luke is not Paul, and we cannot blame him for
that!

The third result of the death of Jesus was, of course, in
Luke's eyes the gift of the Spirit. In one sense we can leave a
full discussion of this on one side here, since it is above all
the material in Acts that is relevant; in any case, we have
already considered some aspects of this already (see too
Marshall 1992: 66-69).

We may note once again that, insofar as this is a study of
Luke's Gospel, the Spirit is mentioned in a surprisingly
uneven way. In part this is due to Luke's salvation-historical
scheme whereby the Spirit is a feature of the post-Easter
situation, the Spirit being the gift of the risen Jesus to the
church (Lk. 24.49). Yet as we have seen, this is not the whole
story at all, since Jesus' own birth is preceded by an outburst
of prophetic activity inspired by the Spirit; Jesus himself is
baptized with the Spirit in Luke 3, he is led by the Spirit into
the desert and then proclaims in Nazareth that he is
anointed by the Spirit for his task as set by God. The gift of
the Spirit is thus a feature of Jesus' ministry quite as much
as of the post-Easter church. Yet, as we have already noted,
references to the Spirit suddenly become very sparse in
Luke's Gospel after ch. 4.

Is it perhaps that Luke assumes that, after his build-up
in chs. 1–4, it is self-evident that everything else in Jesus'
ministry is done in the power of the Spirit? This is possible,
although why Luke should have proceeded so differently
in Acts where the narrative is positively saturated with
references to the working of the Spirit, is not clear.

Conclusion

Luke thus has a rich variety of ways in which to express both
the significance of the person of Jesus and also the relevance

and significance of Jesus' death. Not all of this can be tied down into neat formulae. In part this may be due to Luke's own lack of clarity. In part too it is due to the medium of story, or history, which Luke has chosen as his literary tool to get his message across. Moreover, Luke, as we have seen, is a skilful writer and is sensitive to the story world he is narrating, so that his characters say *appropriate* things: they are not simply transparent windows letting us see Luke and his concerns directly. We must then also be equally sensitive in reading Luke's narrative.

As much, if not more, sensitivity is demanded if we ask how Luke thinks that the Christian life should be conducted in practice and what Luke thought of the significance of Jesus' life and teaching (as opposed to his death). One part of this broad question will form the focus of the next chapter.

Further Reading

C.K. Barrett, 'Theologia Crucis - in Acts?', in C. Andresen and G. Klein (eds.), *Theologia Crucis—Signum Crucis* (FS E. Dinkler; Tübingen: Mohr, 1979), pp. 73-84.

M. de Jonge, 'The Christology of Luke–Acts', in *Christology in Context: The Earliest Christian Responses to Jesus* (Philadelphia: Westminster Press, 1988), pp. 97-111.

C.F. Evans, 'The Central Section of Luke's Gospel', in D.E. Nineham (ed.), *Studies in the Gospels. Essays in Memory of R.H. Lightfoot* (Oxford: Basil Blackwell, 1955), pp. 37-53.

L.T. Johnson, *The Literary Function of Possessions in Luke–Acts* (SBLDS, 39; Missoula, MT: Scholars Press, 1977).

L.E. Keck, 'Toward the Renewal of New Testament Christology', NTS 32 (1986), pp. 362-77, repr. in M.C. de Boer (ed.), *From Jesus to John. Essays on Jesus and New Testament Christology in Honour of Marinus de Jonge* (JSNTSup, 84; Sheffield: JSOT Press, 1993), pp. 321-40.

G.W.H. Lampe, 'The Lucan Portrait of Christ', *NTS* 2 (1956), pp. 160-75.

D.P. Moessner, *Lord of the Banquet. The Literary and Theological Significance of the Lukan Travel Narrative* (Minneapolis: Fortress Press, 1989).

C.F.D. Moule, 'The Christology of Acts', in Keck and Martyn (eds.), *Studies in Luke–Acts*, pp. 159-85.

D.D. Sylva (ed.), Reimagining the Death of the Lukan Jesus (BBB, 73; Frankfurt am Main: Anton Hain, 1990). A collection of essays offering a variety of views.

C.M. Tuckett, 'Atonement in the New Testament', *ABD*, I, pp. 518-22.

—'The Lukan Son of Man', in Tuckett (ed.), *Luke's Literary Achievement* (JSNTSup, 116; Sheffield: JSOT Press, 1995), pp. 198-217.

5

LUKE AND THE CHRISTIAN LIFE: POVERTY AND POSSESSIONS

SO FAR WE HAVE LOOKED at Luke's ideas—on eschatology, on the place of Israel and the Gentiles, and on the significance of the person of Jesus. In very broad terms, this might be called part of Luke's theology. But what of his more concrete, and less abstract, ideas about the implications of the Christian faith? What of his so-called ethics? How is the Christian life to be lived out in practice? And what does the Christian gospel mean for the world? What too is the value of Jesus' teaching given in the Gospel for the present?

Some of these issues might be expected to be answered, if at all, in the book of Acts rather than the Gospel, since Acts does present a picture of Christians actually living out their faith in concrete situations. Certainly some aspects of that living out are clearly emphasized there: the importance of the guidance of the Holy Spirit, evangelism, preaching, prayer etc.

There is, however, one theme which is fairly prominent in (at least some parts of) Acts and is also a major feature of Luke's Gospel. This is the theme of poverty and riches, and possessions or lack of possessions. This theme has often been noted in modern Lukan studies. Indeed it is not just academic studies which have focused on Luke's work in this respect. Luke's Gospel is renowned for having a large amount to say on the topic of riches and poverty. As we shall see, there is a lot of material in Luke that seems to privilege the poor and castigate the rich. Hence for many today who would advocate some kind of a social gospel, with concern to advance the interests of the poor, the persecuted, the exploited and the socially marginalized, the material in Luke has been the part of the New Testament to which they most often appeal. Luke is seen very much as the social gospel, with a bias towards the poor.

Moreover, other aspects of Luke's Gospel are often allied with this concern for the poor. Luke is well known in having a positive attitude to Gentiles (see Chapter 3 above), to women (Lk. 7.11-17; 7.36-50; 8.2-3; 10.38-42; 23.27-31), to tax-collectors and sinners (Lk. 3.12; 5.27-30; 7.29-30, 34, 36-50; 15.1-32; 18.9-14; 19.1-10) and to Samaritans (Lk. 9.52; 10.29-36; 17.10-17). Many have in the past seen all these concerns as simply part of an overall concern on Luke's part for the poor. As we shall see this may in part be the case, but it is by no means self-evident: tax-collectors, for example, were not at all impoverished, nor are all of Luke's women!

The general theme of the poor is prominent in many passages in Luke's Gospel. However, the various traditions recorded by Luke do not all necessarily speak with one voice; nor is it easy to unite Luke and Acts together in this respect, as we shall see. I take first some of the evidence from the Gospel.

The Poor

The poor are clearly stated as the prime objects of Jesus' preaching in the programmatic scene in the synagogue in Nazareth, a story we have referred to already on several occasions: here Jesus proclaims the fulfilment in himself of the text from Isa. 61.1, thereby taking up the announced task to 'bring good news to *the poor*' (Lk. 4.18). Similarly, the teaching of Jesus in Luke's Sermon on the Plain opens with the proclamation in the first beatitude, 'Blessed are you who are poor, for yours in the kingdom of God' (Lk. 6.20); and the messengers of John the Baptist are told by Jesus to go and tell John all the things they have seen and heard: Jesus is performing miracles of healing blindness, deafness, leprosy, even raising the dead, but the climax is the assertion that 'the poor have good news brought to them' (Lk. 7.22 NRSV; perhaps a better translation would be 'the poor are being evangelized'). Similarly, in the Magnificat Mary praises God as the one who 'has brought down the powerful from their thrones, and lifted up the lowly; he has filled the hungry with good things, and sent the rich away empty' (Lk. 1.52-53).

These programmatic statements about the nature of God, and the nature of Jesus' own mission, make it clear that, for Luke, the gospel is indeed primarily one that is for the benefit of the poor.

Critique of the Rich

Coupled with this is a powerful critique of the rich at a number of points. We have already noted the verse from the Magnificat, saying that God is the God who has 'sent the rich away empty' (Lk. 1.53). The beatitude on the poor (6.20) is of course part of a series of beatitudes, probably derived from Q (cf. Mt. 5.3-11). But in Luke, and in Luke alone, the beatitudes are matched by a parallel series of woes (Lk. 6.24-26) so that the blessing on the poor is matched by a corresponding woe: 'Woe to you who are rich, for you have received your consolation' (Lk. 6.24). What is good news for the poor is clearly not good news for those who are not poor.

So too some of the parables in Luke's Gospel are notable for their apparently highly negative attitude to riches: the parable of the rich fool (12.16-21) and the parable of the Rich man and Lazarus (16.19-31) are particularly relevant in this context. Especially in the latter case, the prime reason for the fate of the rich man, in torment in Hades, seems to be solely that in his earthly life he was rich, and in a post-mortem existence earthly roles will be reversed (cf. Lk. 16.25).

Discipleship and Possessions

A notable feature of Luke's Gospel is the way in which he seems to emphasize the fact that Jesus' disciples gave up *everything* they had when they became disciples. Often Luke seems to go out of his way to stress this. Thus the story of the call of Peter in Luke ends with the note that Peter and his companions 'left *everything* and followed him' (Lk. 5.11; the parallel in Mk 1.20 simply has them leaving their homes and following Jesus). Similarly, in the story of the call of Levi, Luke adds to Mark the note that Levi 'left everything' and followed Jesus. (Lk. 5.28 cf. Mk 2.17). The rich young ruler is told in Luke's version of the story to 'sell *all* that you own' (Lk. 18.22: Luke has added the word for 'all' to Mark here: cf. Mk 10.21). Luke records the traditions (from both Mark and Q) of the disciples being sent out on mission by Jesus with virtually no possessions at all (Lk. 9.1-6; 10.1-16: the former is mostly Markan, the latter Q). Finally Luke concludes his double parable of the tower builder and the king going to war with the saying 'None of you can become my disciple if you do not give up all your possessions' (Lk. 14.33). Discipleship in Luke's Gospel seems to involve an even more radical break with one's possessions than is the case in Luke's sources.

Charitable Giving

Coupled with the negative attitude to riches is the strong theme in Luke's writings on the importance of generosity in giving and sharing. Right at the start, Luke (alone of the evangelists) gives the teaching of John the Baptist, advocating generous sharing or giving of goods by those who have plenty to benefit those who have few or none: 'Whoever has two coats must share with anyone who has none; and whoever has food must do likewise' (Lk. 3.11). Similarly, one of the parables peculiar to Luke is the story of the friend at midnight (Lk. 11.5-8) which can be taken, at least on one reading, as a parable encouraging generosity to those in need and a willingness to share one's possessions.

A similar picture emerges from Luke's parable of the Good Samaritan (Lk. 10.29-36, again a parable which appears only in Luke). Whatever the parable may have meant in the pre-Lukan tradition (and one wonders if the fact that the hero of the story is a Samaritan originally had more significance), for Luke it is a clear example of practical charitable action which serves as an example for the listener to imitate. The framework in which the parable is now set is a series of questions or statements about positive action: 'What must I *do*?' asks the lawyer in 10.25; after the exchange about the law including the command to love one's neighbour, Jesus says

'*Do* this and you will live' (v. 28); the man then counters with a further question (about the identity of the neighbour), to which the parable responds, and Jesus' final comment is 'Go and *do* likewise' (v. 37). Whatever the sigificance of the fact that the hero of the story was a Samaritan may have been originally, Luke sees the story as a clear illustration of the importance of direct involvement by helping those in need, if necessary by giving or sharing one's material resources.

This is coupled with a powerful stress on the importance of 'giving alms', or charitable giving, in Luke's Gospel. In Lk. 6.30 Jesus says 'Give to everyone who begs from you'. The word for 'everyone' is absent from Matthew's parallel and may be Luke's addition to Q here. Thus charitable giving is encouraged, and extended to potentially universal scope. In Lk. 11.41 Luke probably rewrites the conclusion of the woe from about purity and cleaning the outside and inside of cups to have Jesus say, 'So *give for alms* those things that are within'. (The quite extraneous nature of the reference to almsgiving makes it likely that Luke has changed Q which is more closely represented by Matthew's 'First clean the inside of the cup' [Mt. 23.26], though the Q version is hard to recover with any certainty.) Similarly, in Lk. 12.33 Luke probably changes Q again by having Jesus exhort the listeners to 'Sell your possessions and *give alms*'. (Again, Matthew's parallel [Mt. 6.19] has no reference to giving alms.) Finally, the story of Zacchaeus (Lk. 19.1-10), a story again peculiar to Luke, ends up with Zacchaeus giving half his possessions to the poor (19.8) in what is in some sense clearly an exemplary act from Luke's point of view.

There is thus a large amount of material in Luke's Gospel indicating a positive attitude to the poor, a rather negative attitude to the rich, an apparently negative attitude at times to possessions, and a strong stress on the importance of giving and sharing on the part of those who are relatively well-off. Moreover, much of this material is either in material peculiar to Luke among the evangelists, or is due to Luke's own redaction of his sources. All this strongly suggests that this concern with the issue is Luke's own at least as much as reflecting any concern from his source materials.

The fact that much of this material, especially the critiques of the rich, appear predominantly in L material has led at least one modern critic (Mealand 1980) to argue that Luke himself may have been not so concerned with this, since it is less easy to document from Luke's redaction of his sources; hence it may be a reflection of a pre-Lukan 'L' stratum of the tradition alone. This is possible, though one must remember that (a) Luke's redaction has not been inactive in stressing the importance of lack of possessions, especially by disciples (cf. above), and (b) we cannot drive too much of a wedge between Luke and his traditions (see p. 26 above): hence even if some of the L material on poverty is not a redactional creation *de novo* by Luke, the fact that Luke has decided to include it in his Gospel is still of significance in telling us something about Luke's own interests. Thus in what follows I shall assume that this theme is an important one for Luke, not just for a pre-Lukan stratum of the tradition.

It is apparent, however, that not all of the material considered is quite of the same nature, nor does it all point the same way in relation to wealth, poverty, possessions or asceticism. Some parts seem to indicate an almost absolute rejection of the value and importance of money and material possessions; other parts seem only to encourage a willingness to share some of the excesses one may enjoy. For example, in relation to possessions and money, the disciples of Jesus are apparently expected to—and do—give up everything; and yet some of the teaching on almsgiving and sharing presupposes that people do still have possessions over which they retain control.

The situation becomes even more confusing if we ask the question how far all this is considered by Luke to be still applicable to the Christians of his own day, or even if we try to bring in the evidence of Acts to supplement the evidence of the Gospel.

The Evidence of Acts

The evidence of Acts is certainly rather confusing and not clear. The early chapters of Acts (Acts 1–5) present a picture of the primitive church in Jerusalem in one sense obeying the radical calls for renunciation by the Lukan Jesus: the disciples have nothing they can call their own individual property and they hold everything in common, used for the common good (2.44-45; 4.32-35).

However, even within these chapters, there is some inconsistency as to whether this was a universally practised phenomenon within the Christian community (as the summaries just cited seem to imply), or whether people only sold some of their surplus, and moreover did so on a voluntary basis (as seems to be implied by the note about Barnabas selling his field in Acts 4.36, and the story about Ananias and Sapphira in Acts 5.1-11: the sin of the latter is not that they have kept some of their possessions for themselves, but that they have not been honest in telling others what they have done).

What is perhaps more surprising is that, after the first five chapters in Acts, the situation seems to change. The economic set-up of the primitive Jerusalem church is not replicated in other communities founded by the Christian mission; the Christians themselves do not give up all their possessions, and in fact the story presupposes that the Christians have quite a lot of material means at their disposal to finance all the various comings and goings that take place. The church seems to include various people who may have had considerable means (cf. the proconsul Sergius Paulus in Acts 13.1, Lydia who was 'a dealer in purple cloth' in 16.14, or the reference to 'not a few Greek women and men of high standing' in Beroea in 17.12 etc., none of whom appear to give up their possessions). Further, there is absolutely nothing in the way Luke tells the story in Acts to suggest that the economic arrangements in the later churches represent a disastrous come-down from the glorious golden days of the first community.

Yet despite this discrepancy within Luke–Acts as a whole, which is very real, it should also be noted that some themes remain important throughout Luke's story. This applies especially to the evident importance for Luke of charitable giving. On a number of occasions in Acts, individuals who are evidently regarded as paradigms of virtue in the story are described in terms of their activity in giving generously. For example, Cornelius was 'a devout man who feared God with all his household; *he gave alms generously* to the people and prayed constantly to God' (Acts 10.2). Tabitha in Joppa 'was devoted to good works and *acts of charity*' (9.36). Paul defends himself before Felix by saying that he came to Jerusalem '*to bring alms* to my nation and to offer sacrifices' (24.17: this is Luke's only—and very oblique—reference to the great collection organized by Paul among the Gentile churches for the Jerusalem church).

Finally we should note that, although (perhaps strangely) the Christians in the story in Acts hardly ever refer to the teaching of Jesus in their own preaching, the one exception is when Paul cites a saying of Jesus (*not* recorded in Luke's, or any other, Gospel) that 'It is more blessed to give than to receive' (Acts 20.35). Thus at least the theme of charitable giving is one that retains its importance throughout Luke's two-volume work.

Yet even here we can see some differences between the Gospel and Acts. In the Gospel, giving seems to be encouraged for the benefit of the poor in general. In Acts it is predominantly the Christian poor who receive bounty from more well-to-do Christians. Christians in Acts do not go around helping the poor and needy outside their own ranks. Christian charity seems to be rather strictly 'in-house'.

What though are we to make of the more radical elements in Luke's Gospel, the parts which seem to imply and demand a total renunciation of all goods and possessions of any would-be follower of Jesus, and the stinging attacks on the rich simply apparently because they are rich?

It seems hard to deny that Luke does not regard the elements of his Gospel, apparently insisting on radical and total renunciation of all property and possessions, as essential for Christian discipleship after the time of Jesus. The story in Acts seems quite clear on this: the deafening silence of a total absence of any critique of Christians' still having money and property throughout so much of Acts makes this fairly clear. Indeed it may be explicitly signalled by Luke in his Gospel. In a passage peculiar to Luke, Jesus speaks to the twelve, and refers to the mission instructions given earlier in the Gospel (in fact the instruction given to the 70!), asking them 'When I sent you out without a purse, bag or sandals, did you lack anything?' (Lk. 22.35). When they reply

'No, not a thing', Jesus says 'But now, the one who has a purse must take it, and likewise a bag. And the one who has no sword must sell his cloak and buy one' (v. 36). It looks as if Luke's Jesus is consciously signalling a change in the circumstances of Christian disciples: the model of radical renunciation applies during the time of Jesus, but in Luke's day the situation is different: Christians will have possessions, even if they are expected to use them circumspectly and generously.

Who are the Poor?

Before we go further, we need to ask perhaps what Luke actually understands by 'poverty'. Who are 'the poor' in Luke's eyes?

The situation is complicated by different meanings of the word for 'poor' (Greek *ptōchos*) in different contexts. Very broadly speaking, the Hellenistic world used the word 'poor' to refer to those in social and economic poverty, indeed usually in situations of very extreme poverty. The 'poor' are thus the materially deprived, the financially destitute. In Judaism, this language is also used; but alongside it there develops a slightly different usage. The materially poor and destitute are of course the object of God's concern and care in the Old Testament; this then leads to the idea that the poor are those who rely totally on God in utter dependence for their existence. The poor are thus the humble, the pious. Hence in Judaism the language develops whereby the 'poor' are equally those who are spiritually poor, those who are humble before God, the pious, and in some contexts this idea supplanted the reference to the 'poor' as the materially destitute. 'Poverty' can then be seen as a term denoting religious attitude, as much as, or at times instead of, material destitution.

We may see such vocabulary being used in Isa. 61.1, where the prophet announces good news to the 'poor', perhaps meaning the humble and pious. Matthew seems to have taken some of the language about poverty in this way, so that for example his version of the first beatitude is 'Blessed are the poor *in spirit*' (Mt. 5.3), meaning the humble and pious, those who are poor before God.

What though of Luke? Certainly the material and economic side of 'poverty' is never lost in Luke's understanding. The contrasts set up between the 'poor' and the 'rich' (Lk. 6.20, 24), or the beatitude in Lk. 6.21 which speaks of the 'hungry' (Matthew has those who 'hunger and thirst after righteousness', Mt. 5.6), and contrasts them with those who are physically full in the corresponding woe (Lk. 6.25), make it clear that material situations are in mind. The illustrations of the poor in the parables such as the Rich Man and Lazarus (16.19-31) also indicate that in many respects poverty is material, economic and financial poverty, not spiritual poverty. Even the quotation of Isaiah 61 in Luke 4 makes it fairly clear that, for Luke at least (and perhaps unlike the author of Isa. 61 itself), the recipients of the good news are the materially poor.

On the other hand, the idea of a less material kind of poverty is not absent from Luke. The diatribe of the Magnificat against the 'rich' and the promise to the 'hungry' (1.53) is set in parallel to the claim that God has exalted not the 'poor' but the 'lowly' (1.52 NRSV) or 'humble'. Those who are 'hungry' and suffering are also for Luke the 'humble' and pious.

Conversely, the attacks on the rich in Luke need to be read carefully. The parable of the rich fool (12.16-21) is very revealing. The fool is portrayed as the one who has wealth and makes provision for the future. But the punch line at the end does not just condemn the possession of riches as such. Jesus says 'So it is with those who store up treasures for themselves *but are not rich towards God*' (v. 21). It is thus not so much, or not only, riches and possessions as such that is crucial: it is the attitude of the person towards God.

One modern writer has even gone so far as to suggest that possessions and money in Luke's story operate almost as a cipher for one's attitude to God and/or Jesus: 'the expressions rich and poor function within the story as metaphorical expressions for those‘ rejected and accepted because of their response to the prophet' (Johnson 1977: 140). In its most literal form this is probably too extreme, since Luke does not lose sight of the idea of economic and material poverty as well (as Johnson himself fully acknowledges in his study).

Nevertheless, it is an important aspect of Luke's overall
presentation of the theme of poverty in his writings.

Luke: The Rich and the Poor

What though of the material side of things? As was the case
when we considered Luke and Judaism, quite a lot depends
on how one envisages Luke's situation. To put it crudely, is
Luke addressing a community that is rich or a community
that is poor? Are the tirades against the rich meant as a cry
of frustration from a poverty-stricken community, produced
in a way similar to the way in which many have argued
apocalyptic traditions are used by disadvantaged and/or
persecuted groups to try to come to terms with their present
situation and give hope for the future? Or are the exhortations to poverty directed at people who are reasonably
affluent as a critique of their present lifestyle? Or is it a
matter of both?

   The trend in recent Lukan studies has been to argue that
Luke is addressing a community that is certainly partly,
maybe dominantly and perhaps even exclusively, quite well-
to-do in material terms. Certainly there is quite a lot of
material suggesting this. For example, Luke mentions the
women who helped Jesus in his ministry (one of whom comes
from Herod's household) and who evidently have sufficient
material resources to support Jesus and his followers
(Lk. 8.3). In Acts, as we have seen, Christian followers and
sympathizers often appear as reasonably well-to-do: the
Ethiopian eunuch (Acts 8.26-40), Manaen who is a member
of Herod's court (13.1), the pro-consul Sergius Paulus (13.7),
the people of 'high standing' in Beroea (17.12) etc.

   Moreover, much of the material in Luke's Gospel on the
topic of money etc. is clearly directed at those who have possessions, for example, the exhortations to give generously
(Lk. 6.30, 35; 11.41; 12.33-34) which we have already noted
and which would be somewhat precious if addressed to those
who are destitute. So too the parable of the rich fool is
addressed to those with riches. The parable of the Rich man
and Lazarus gives the lion's share of attention in the story to
the rich man and his fate: Lazarus, despite his having a

name, is a very minor character and in many ways simply a foil to drive home the lesson of the story about the rich man. The context in which the parable of the Great Supper is placed by Luke is one of teaching about who should be invited to meals (Lk. 14.12-14); again this would be at best precious if addressed to the destitute who cannot feed themselves, let alone provide dinner parties. Similarly, the exhortation at the end of the parable of the unjust steward (Lk. 16.1-8), to 'make friends for yourselves by means of mammon [i.e. wealth]' (v. 9) clearly has in view those with money, not those without.

It seems very likely that Luke is, at least in part, addressing Christians who are certainly not materially destitute, but reasonably affluent. As such then, Luke's picture presents demands on the rich to use their money wisely and properly, and to give generously to those in need (see Karris 1978; Stegemann 1986).

Nevertheless, the other side of things cannot be ignored. Esler has argued that the general social mix found in any Hellenistic city of the time would indicate that the poor, that is, the destitute, were also a part of the Christian community, and that a mixture of the extremes of financial and social situations may be reflected in the stories of Elijah and Elisha helping the impoverished widow and the relatively well-to-do Naaman respectively (Lk. 4.25-27). Hence the Lukan community may have been socially very mixed. The same may be shown by the parable of the Great Supper, told by Jesus, according to Luke, to exhort the hearers to invite not only their social equals who could respond in kind, but also their social (and financial) inferiors who could never respond in kind (Lk. 14.12-14). According to Esler, this may also then reflect the situation of Luke's community, with table fellowship at the *same* table being strongly urged on all members of the community, especially on those whose social position was such that they would not normally engage in such practice.

This is possible, though one must also note that much of the conversation seems to be rather one-sided: the exhortations are constantly to the rich, the influential and those with possessions. In one sense this is inevitable since the poor, precisely by virtue of their poverty, are in a position of total powerlessness and cannot do anything either for themselves or for others. Nevertheless, the powerful arguments and exhortations directed to the rich do suggest that Luke's community may have been predominantly reasonably well-to-do.

It may be too in this light that Luke's portrait of the disciples should be read. As we have seen, Jesus' disciples during his lifetime adopt a lifestyle of material and financial renunciation that is far more radical than that reflected in Acts. Perhaps though, in part, this picture—which is not peculiar to Luke since it is there in his sources, but is certainly developed by him—is intended as a challenge and a critique for richer Christians of Luke's own day. The disciples are not necessarily role models to be imitated precisely. As we have seen, Luke is aware that the era of Jesus now lies in the past; perhaps too then the same applies to the model of discipleship as seen in the Gospel stories. Yet the picture painted by Luke can still serve as a powerful image of the total commitment, and the potential renunciation, which Christians in his own day may have been called to make.

We should also note that for Luke, poverty as such is not an ideal. The poor and the needy in Luke are not told that their life of freedom from property and material goods is itself true happiness. Luke then is no Cynic philosopher, preaching the value of detachment from the cares of this world. The hungry and the needy are promised that their needs will be satisfied (Lk. 6.21). Even when the disciples practise their radical lifestyle, we are told that they in fact did not suffer materially (22.35), presumably because others gave them what they needed. Luke's positive picture of renunciation by the disciples during Jesus' lifetime is thus in no way promoting an ascetic ideal. The poor are promised that a better future lies ahead. Similarly, in Acts, any ideal in the model of the economic set-up of the primitive Jerusalem church does not lead to a life of asceticism: any money that is available is pooled and used, not given away to third parties.

Moreover, for Luke the good news which is promised to the poor is by no means simply an other-worldly hope for a better time that will come in a future life. Such an idea is not lacking (cf. Lk. 16.19-31), but Luke also has a firm idea that the Gospel has—or should have—real concrete implications for the poor in this world. (The point is strongly emphasized by Esler 1987: 193-97.) The blessings announced in the Nazareth sermon, including sight for the blind and release of the captives, are enacted by Luke's Jesus (cf. Lk. 13.10-17; 18.35-43). The feeding of the hungry takes place in Jesus' feeding of the 5000 (Lk. 9.10-17). The good news for the poor is shown to have practical consequences for the really poor in the picture of the early church in Acts where no one is in need and everything is shared (Acts 2.44-46; 4.32-37, cf. especially v. 34: 'There was not a needy person among them'). Thus despite an undoubted other-worldly element in the promises for the poor, Luke's story shows that the gospel can, and should, lead to a changed reality in this world. Luke's Gospel is thus a promise to the poor of a change in their fortunes, as well as a challenge to the rich to bring that change about.

Reversal

The whole matter of poverty or riches may be part of a still wider and more inclusive theme in Luke–Acts. This is the thesis of the recent study of York (1991): the theme of riches/poverty is part of a more all-embracing scheme of *reversal* in Luke, covering not only money but more importantly status, worth and value, or, to use the language adopted by some social anthropologists in relation to biblical texts seen in the context of the Mediterranean world, honour and shame.

If we look once again at the parable of the Great Supper and its context in Luke, the poor are coupled with 'the crippled, the lame, and the blind' as the people whom one should invite and share a table with (Lk. 14.13, cf. also v. 21 and 7.22). But these are not only the people who are financially destitute; they are also those who are excluded from participating in the Jewish cult (cf. Lev. 21.18): they are thus the *social* outcasts, the people who have no honour in the eyes of the respectable and well-to-do. They are unable to repay any hospitality (and so bring any return of honour to the host);

and being in positions of shame themselves, they provide no
honour to a benefactor who would seek to become a patron
for them. What is recommended is thus the exact antithesis
of any seeking of honour for oneself in such an honour–
shame society. What is demanded is not only an ending of
financial and economic hardship (though this is part of
things), but also a deeper re-evaluation of what is to count as
honour, as worthy of recognition and what is not. As often as
not, the gospel brings about a *reversal* of previously held
human values, and certainly a strong condemnation of any
attempt to establish or to enhance one's own honour in the
sight of others.

York seeks to show that this theme of reversal pervades
the whole of Luke's narrative at a very deep level. It not only
surfaces in the riches/poverty theme, but also in the sayings
about being humbled and exalted (Lk. 14.11; 18.14), and in
parables such as the Pharisee and the tax-collector (18.9-13).
Here the issue is not clearly one of rich against poor: the
Pharisee is not necessarily rich, and the tax-collector is
almost certainly the very opposite of poor in material terms.
Yet like the rich/poor antithesis, we see here a not unrelated
total reversal of the value systems of other human beings, so
that what counts as honour and worth in the eyes of men and
women is shown to be reversed in God's eyes. Thus, to return
to one of the points with which we started this chapter, the
poor and the tax-collectors *may* be on a par in Luke's story,
not necessarily because tax-collectors were destitute (they
were not!), but because both lack honour in a culture dominated by the categories of honour and shame. The gospel is
then not only good news for the economically poor, but also
good news for those without any honour in society, in
proclaiming the reversal of such human values in the sight of
God.

York's study raises some very interesting ideas. Not all of
his argument is equally persuasive. It is, for example, not
always clear how far Luke is advocating a reversal of the
whole value system, the whole set of criteria for attributing
honour/shame (as for example in the parable of the Pharisee
and the tax-collector) and how far Luke's Jesus is simply
adopting the current criteria to critique just selfishness. For

example, neither the rich fool who does not use his money and wealth to benefit others, nor the rich man in relation to Lazarus, would be accorded honour in the honour–shame culture as outlined by York (in dependence on the work of Malina and others) simply because they refused to share their wealth with others. Benefaction in such a society was highly regarded; self-interested hoarding was not. Any reversal here is perhaps not as fundamental as in Lk. 18.9-13 or 14.12-14. Nevertheless, York's work shows the value—and the importance—of extending the parameters of the discussion to include insights from social anthropology and sociology, as well as the more limited, traditional categories used by biblical exegetes to throw light upon the text.

Conclusion

We have focused in this chapter on just one aspect of the Christian life, and of the teaching of Jesus in Luke's Gospel, as shown in the Lukan writings. As we have seen, the picture is a complex one. In part, no doubt, this is due once again to Luke's sensitivity as a story-teller, or as a history-teller. Luke writes as a historian and he is thus aware that the events he narrates are in the past. He knows too that not everything said in the past can be transferred to a later time without alteration. Thus the model of discipleship which Luke develops in his Gospel is, in at least one respect anyway, not a model which is repeated after the time of Jesus: disciples no longer give up *everything* when they become believers. Luke is thus aware of the distance between his own day and the time of Jesus. The story world he creates cannot simply be applied without thought to the real world of his own day.

Luke thus shows himself to be perhaps surprisingly modern in this. In dealing with traditions from the past which Luke no doubt thinks are of great importance for his present, one cannot just ignore the difference between past and present and pretend that the past speaks to the present simply by repeating the same words which can then be understood in the present's terms without more ado. It is to some of these hermeneutical reflections that we shall turn in the final chapter.

Further Reading

P.F. Esler, *Community and Gospel in Luke–Acts* (SNTSMS, 57; Cambridge: Cambridge University Press, 1987).

L.T. Johnson, *The Literary Function of Possessions in Luke–Acts* (SBLDS, 39; Missoula, MT: Scholars Press, 1977).

R.J. Karris, 'Poor and Rich: The Lukan *Sitz im Leben*', in Talbert (ed.), *Perspectives on Luke–Acts*, pp. 112-25.

D.L. Mealand, *Poverty and Expectation in the Gospels* (London: SPCK, 1980).

T.E. Schmidt, *Hostility to Wealth in the Synoptic Gospels* (JSNTSup, 15; Sheffield: JSOT Press, 1987), esp. ch. 7, 'Hostility to Wealth in the Gospel of Luke', pp. 135-62.

W. Stegemann, 'The Following of Christ as Solidarity between Rich, Respected Christians and Poor, Despised Christians (Gospel of Luke)', in L. Schottroff and W. Stegemann, *Jesus and the Hope of the Poor* (ET; Marynoll, NY: Orbis Books, 1986), pp. 67-120.

J.O. York, *The Last shall be First: The Rhetoric of Reversal in Luke* (JSNTSup, 46; Sheffield: JSOT Press, 1991).

6

CONCLUDING HERMENEUTICAL REFLECTIONS

IN THE PREVIOUS CHAPTERS, I have tried to look at some of the problems surrounding the interpretation of the Gospel of Luke, viewed as an ancient text. The approach has been, broadly speaking, a historical-critical one: by this I mean that the attempt has been made to view the text in, and as part of, its original setting in history. With regard to a text which is giving an account of events prior to its time of writing, there are of course peculiar problems. Does original refer to the time of the story, or to the time of the writing of the text? How far should one focus on the events of the story, and how far on the author and his/her situation? Nevertheless, the historical nature of the text is important, even if we begin to bracket off some of these historical questions and begin to analyse the text as a literary whole in its own right.

Few would want to go so far as to ignore historical questions completely. We have to understand the language of the text—and that involves placing the text in a historical linguistic context (in this case the Greek speaking world of the late first century CE). We have to know something of the background against which we can and should appropriately understand key words and phrases. (It would, I suggest, be quite wrong to take Luke's language of Jesus as 'Son of God' as meaning exactly what the Council of Chalcedon meant by the same words without ever worrying about the issue of possible anachronism.) We also need to know something about the social realities of the context of the text. Often in our quest, the insights from other academic disciplines, such as sociology or social anthropology, can help to throw important light on the text (as we saw in relation to legitimation, or in relation to Luke's ideas on reversal). Often too we would like to know more than we in fact do about key aspects of the context of the text which would affect the interpretation significantly: for example, the author's Jewishness, or non-Jewishness, might affect our assessment of what the text says about Jews and Judaism very significantly, as we saw. But all these historical issues are vitally important in our understanding of Luke's Gospel, just as in the case of any text from antiquity.

However, Luke's text is not quite like any other text from antiquity. Whether we like it or not, the fact is that this text we have been studying is a *Gospel*, a book which has its place in a Christian Bible, and as such is part of the sacred Scripture of the Christian church. For many people, therefore, and indeed for many people studying this text within an academic context, the text has religious significance for their own contemporary religious faith. Luke's Gospel is to be seen not only as an ancient text but also as a text which it is believed is still relevant (in some way) for the present and still speaks to the present.

The previous paragraph could of course have been written about any book of the New Testament. In the case of Luke's Gospel, the situation is even more acute, since a Gospel gives an account of the life and teaching of Jesus, and for the Christian faith, the person of Jesus is of absolutely central significance. The interpretation of a Gospel thus raises vital hermeneutical issues for many people. Such issues raise profound questions, though these can only be discussed here in a very superficial way—partly for reasons of space, partly for reasons of expertise. So what is offered here is only a very brief, and naïve, set of suggestions.

For many people, the teaching of Jesus is central to contemporary Christian faith and morality. In relation to the interpretation of Luke's Gospel, one must say that, *if* one's concern is to recover the teaching of the historical Jesus on this or that topic, then Luke's Gospel may be a means to that end, but it is not that end in itself. It is certainly a means to that end. Some of the L material, especially the parables, may give us very important aspects of Jesus' teaching which would otherwise not be available to us. But Luke's Gospel certainly does not give us a pure, unadulterated account of the teaching of Jesus. We have seen a number of occasions where Luke has almost certainly *changed* his tradition (whether Mark or Q, or perhaps even one of his other sources). Luke adds things to Mark here, changes Q there, alters a saying here, omits a story there etc. If we want the pure, unadulterated teaching of Jesus (if such an aim could ever be realized!), then we shall have to make full allowances for the things Luke has done to his traditions. We certainly cannot simply read Luke's Gospel as if it were an exact transcript of the life or teaching of Jesus. In reading Luke's Gospel, therefore, we see *Luke's* Jesus, not the pure unvarnished Jesus.

Although many starting critical studies of the Gospel find this a little difficult to accept at first, there are real questions to ask about whether this should be regarded as all loss. There are immense problems about ever succeeding in recovering the pure unvarnished Jesus of history. But even if we could, some would argue that this is not necessarily as central for Christian faith as others would claim. Certainly the early Christians might have argued in this way. What was important for them was not so much a voice from the past as rigid and unchanging, giving timeless, fixed and unalterable dogmas or ethical instructions which would never change to all eternity. The early Christians believed, rightly or wrongly, that the Jesus of history, the Jesus who had come from Nazareth and had been crucified, had been in some profound sense raised by God in a unique way and was now alive and present with his people, enabling them to be guided and inspired in their lives in ways they had never experienced before. It was, they believed, the same Jesus who had lived among them (or their predecessors) in Palestine; and that in part was no doubt one of the reasons why traditions found now in our Gospels were preserved. But this same Jesus was now the source and inspiration which was leading them into new areas and in new ways.

In all this Luke seems to have been no exception. Luke
was, of course, unlike many other Christians of his time.
Very few wrote books; even fewer wrote Gospels; and no one
else wrote an equivalent of Acts. So too Luke's idea of the
guiding presence of Jesus in the post-Easter church is far
more of an indirect presence than, say, Paul's: for Luke,
Jesus is alive in heaven, and the guiding action on earth is
more the work of the Holy Spirit than of Jesus directly. Yet
Luke shows us, perhaps more so than some other New
Testament writers, that the Christian gospel can be, and
perhaps should be, adapted to changing circumstances.

We have already noted on a number of occasions what I
have called Luke's sensitivity or literary skill: Luke takes
some care at times not to write back too much of his own
ideas into his story. He lets the characters of his story say
their thing in their own way, and this may apply to Jesus in
the Gospel quite as much as to characters like Peter or Paul
in Acts. Luke has his own agenda—that is clear. But he does
not always write it back into his story world. All this means
in one way that we can perhaps have greater confidence in
Luke as a reliable historian: he certainly tries to report many
things accurately (even if his level of success may have been
variable!).

But the other side of the coin is perhaps equally significant
in the present context. Luke realizes that there is a difference between past and present. We saw this, for example, in
relation to eschatology. Thus, as we have said, the present is
not read into the past without more ado. But then the past
cannot simply be translated into the present without ado
either. Luke's agenda, and Luke's vocabulary, are no doubt
very real for him: but they are not necessarily the same as
the agenda and the vocabulary of the past. We have seen this
at more than one level and in relation to more than one
issue. In relation to Judaism, the battles and disputes which
take place in Luke's story are not necessarily the battles and
disputes in which he himself is engaged. The ethical stance
of the Gospel in relation, say, to discipleship and possessions
is not quite the same as that of his own day, or even as that
of Acts: the instructions of the Gospel are *not* timeless
unchanging words which can be repeated ever anew in

changed situations. The words, if they are to be applied in the present, may have to be changed. Indeed, Luke's Jesus does this quite explicitly in relation to the question of possessions and discipleship (cf. Lk. 22.35).

Luke does little explicitly to show how this change takes place. He shows himself to be surprisingly modern in his awareness of the gap between his own time and the past—a gap which is certainly historical, perhaps cultural as well, perhaps hermeneutical. Yet he does not do so much to tell us how he bridges that gap, let alone how others might bridge it. Nevertheless it is clear that a real amount of bridging is going on. Luke does not tell his story just for fun. He does not write for his own amusement. Writing in the ancient world was a time-consuming and expensive business. Luke writes because he believes that his history will have a relevance to his own situation—but perhaps in a less direct way than others have envisaged. His Gospel story of Jesus, privileging the poor, castigating the rich, and having disciples who give up everything, does not necessarily set up a blueprint for his own day. Rather, it seeks to challenge a status quo that is perhaps becoming too complacent. So too his picture of Judaism may serve a number of aims, one of which is to unite the Christian church firmly to its Jewish roots.

For a modern Christian reader of Luke's work, one can perhaps pay him the greatest compliment if one is prepared to follow in his footsteps of *not* simply transferring the words of his Gospel to quite different situations and expecting them to have an unchanging, eternal significance and meaning. An elementary understanding of semantics should have warned us against this anyway: words change their meaning when placed in different contexts, and can never have the eternal, immutable meaning for which some would vainly hope.

There is no doubt that Luke's picture of Jesus can, and does, challenge many today. The Jesus who challenges the rich and affluent of his day also challenges a world such as our own, with glaring social and economic inequalities. Few who go to church in the Western world can hear the parable of the Rich Man and Lazarus with any comfort today. The Jesus whose story is so profoundly rooted in the Jewish faith and the Jewish community must surely challenge a

Christian church which bears his name but which is so separated from contemporary Judaism. The Jesus of Luke's story,
whose ethic is so practical and down-to-earth in helping
those in need, must surely challenge any would-be followers
to be equally practical and down-to-earth in the practice of
their religion.

Yet how all this might work out in practice is never spelt
out—and perhaps wisely so—by Luke. Luke does not even
carry over the words of the teaching of the Gospel into his
story in Acts: as we noted in passing earlier, Jesus' words of
the Gospel are never cited in Acts. (There is only one saying
of Jesus cited [Acts 20.35] and that is not a saying recorded
in Luke's Gospel.)

There is not a little justification for Luke's silence in not
spelling out the hermeneutical moves he might have made,
or at least not recording them for posterity. The hermeneutical task, of reappropriating the tradition and applying it to
ever new situations, is a task which can only be undertaken
by the individuals and groups themselves in their own situations. Luke's economic model (if that is what it is) of the set-
up in the primitive Jerusalem church would not necessarily
apply in a post-industrial modern city. Nor would it really
address the deeper societal problems which create, and
perpetuate, inequality, deprivation and poverty in the first
place. Someone else's solution, in a different social situation,
cannot simply be transformed to a new social context and
remain unchanged. A corollary must be that what is a solution in one context will not necessarily succeed in another.
For example, Luke's solution to the problem posed by the
eschatological teaching in his traditions, seeking to reassert
the teaching of an imminent End in the face of delay, can
scarcely be ours, living nearly 2000 years later. Similarly,
however powerful in general terms the teaching of the Lukan
Jesus on poverty may be for a situation of the gross inequalities that characterize our world today, few would probably
feel happy with Luke's own apparent interpretation of that
teaching in his story in Acts which seems to envisage practical action for the relief of poverty being restricted to benefit
poor Christians only.

Luke's Jesus is a challenging Jesus for those who live in

relative affluence. But Luke himself is a challenging writer too. His implied hermeneutic means that he hands nothing to his readers on a plate. Or rather, what he hands on is his account of the past in a history. He, in his day, struggles to make that history relevant to his own situation. Those for whom Luke's writings now form part of a canon of Scripture have an obligation to make the same struggle; but the easy option of a biblical fundamentalism which simply repeats the words from the past is not, one suspects, Luke's preferred option. For Luke, the church goes forward in the power of the Holy Spirit, ever conscious of its past and tied irrevocably to his roots, but seeking too to change and adapt to the new situations in which it finds itself. The struggle to maintain the balance between the past and the future is part of the challenge which Luke's writings pose for every generation of Christians.

Further Reading

N. Lash, 'What Might Martyrdom Mean?', in W. Horbury and B. McNeil (eds.), *Suffering and Martyrdom in the New Testament* (Cambridge: Cambridge University Press, 1981), pp. 183-98.

R. Morgan and J. Barton, *Biblical Interpretation* (Oxford: Oxford University Press, 1988).

C.M. Tuckett, *Reading the New Testament* (London: SPCK, 1987).

INDEXES

INDEX OF REFERENCES

INDEX OF AUTHORS